LIGHT COME SHINING

INNER LIVES

SERIES EDITOR
William Todd Schultz

———

Dan P. Mcadams
GEORGE W. BUSH AND THE REDEMPTIVE DREAM:
A PSYCHOLOGICAL PORTRAIT

William Todd Schultz
TINY TERROR: WHY TRUMAN CAPOTE (ALMOST)
WROTE ANSWERED PRAYERS

Tim Kasser
LUCY IN THE MIND OF LENNON

Kyle Arnold
THE DIVINE MADNESS OF PHILIP K. DICK

Andrew McCarron
LIGHT COME SHINING: THE TRANSFORMATIONS
OF BOB DYLAN

LIGHT COME SHINING

The Transformations of Bob Dylan

Andrew McCarron

OXFORD
UNIVERSITY PRESS

OXFORD
UNIVERSITY PRESS

Oxford University Press is a department of the University of Oxford. It furthers
the University's objective of excellence in research, scholarship, and education
by publishing worldwide. Oxford is a registered trade mark of Oxford University
Press in the UK and certain other countries.

Published in the United States of America by Oxford University Press
198 Madison Avenue, New York, NY 10016, United States of America.

Library of Congress Cataloging-in-Publication Data
Names: McCarron, Andrew, author.
Title: Light come shining : the transformations of Bob Dylan / Andrew McCarron.
Description: New York : Oxford University Press, 2017. | Includes bibliographical
references.
Identifiers: LCCN 2016006379 | ISBN 9780199313471 (hardback: alk. paper)
Subjects: LCSH: Dylan, Bob, 1941– | Singers—United States—Biography. |
Dylan, Bob, 1941—Psychology. | Singers—United States—Psychology.
Classification: LCC ML420.D98 M176 2017 | DDC 782.42164092—dc23
LC record available at http://lccn.loc.gov/2016006379

9 8 7 6 5 4 3 2
Printed by Sheridan Books, Inc., United States of America

CONTENTS

CREDITS

A Hard Rain's A-Gonna Fall
Copyright © 1963 by Warner Bros. Inc.; renewed 1991 by Special Rider Music

Ain't Talkin'
Copyright © 2006 by Special Rider Music

Ballad Of A Thin Man
Copyright © 1965 by Warner Bros. Inc.; renewed 1993 by Special Rider Music

Dark Eyes
Copyright © 1985 by Special Rider Music

Desolation Row
Copyright © 1965 by Warner Bros. Inc.; renewed 1993 by Special Rider Music

Every Grain Of Sand
Copyright © 1981 by Special Rider Music

I Shall Be Released
Copyright ©1967, 1970 by Dwarf Music; renewed 1995 by Dwarf Music

PROLOGUE

A CASE FOR THIS PSYCHOBIOGRAPHY

And not the lifetime of one man only
But of old stones that cannot be deciphered

—T. S. Eliot

Why a psychobiography on Bob Dylan, especially considering the staggering number of Dylan books out in the world? Is there more to be known? Hasn't everything been said already? To be sure, several outstanding biographies exist. Robert Shelton's pioneering *No Direction Home* (1986, 2010), Howard Sounes's scrupulously researched *Down the Highway* (2001, 2011), and, easily the best of all, Clinton Heylin's ever-expanding *Behind the Shades* (1991, 2001, 2011) offer excellent portraits of the enigmatic rock star. There is also a sizable library of Dylan books with a topical focus. Whether it's the folkies of Greenwich Village, the student movement of the Sixties and Seventies, Born Again Christians, the Chabad Lubavitch community, or English Department postmodernists, specific intellectual and sociopolitical groups have repeatedly claimed Bob Dylan as their spokesperson or guru. It's not uncommon to encounter books that make a case for a philosophical center to Dylan's oeuvre, or a Jewish one, or an Anglo poetic foundation. There are also unpublished manuscripts decrying him as an overrated plagiarizing drunkard with few friends,[1] as well as saintly accounts that have him doing everything short of multiplying loaves and walking on water.

And then there are the many blogs and fanzines dedicated to "Bob's" every set list and public appearance, and obsessive fans who have done everything from dig through his garbage to buy his boyhood home, ostensibly for posterity, but just as likely to maintain tenuous connections to a man they've never met yet feel they know intimately. In *The Dylanologists* (2014), author David Kinney explores the life stories of a group of these obsessive fans, some of whom have dedicated large chunks of their lives to following Dylan's tour bus and traveling on pilgrimages to places that are significant to his legend—Hibbing, the Kettle of Fish and Café Wha? in Greenwich Village, and Woodstock, among other locations. Early in his book, Kinney offers a description of this bizarre subculture within which he includes himself:

> We keep track of everything: every recording session and every tour date, every song on every bootleg, every word ever caught by a recording device. We are all preoccupied with facts and dates, as if cataloguing these things will solve the mysteries of his life, and ours. We investigate the unanswered questions of his career. We pile up pages for Dylan books and Dylan fanzines and Dylan blogs, or just for our

1. In the late 1990s, Dylan's former girlfriend, Susan Ross, unsuccessfully attempted to find a publisher for a tell-all unauthorized biography of her ex-boyfriend that revealed him to be a lousy lover and raging alcoholic who'd been secretly married twice and fathered a number of children since his 1978 divorce from his first wife Sara Lownds.

own private circle of Dylan friends. We go to conventions and tribute shows and meet-ups and lectures. We figure out how to play the songs on our guitars. We track down all the literary, musical, and cultural allusions in his work. We collect the things he left behind: scraps of writing paper, guitars, harmonicas, books, cigarette butts. One day we discover with a flash that more than a few of our closest friends, sometimes even our spouses, are fellow fans. (Kinney, 2014, 2)

The projections of biographers, experts, and other interpreters have generated a kaleidoscopic public image that has burdened and frustrated the living and breathing man beyond any conceivable measure (in addition to making him a great deal of money). According to Dylan's Greenwich Village girlfriend, Suze Rotolo, Dylan's followers are so taken by his music that they make him in their own image. Consequently, the sprawling literature that has sprung up around him has increased his multiplicity, mystery, and elusiveness. Finding the man in the myth requires an approach akin to what the German theologian Rudolf Bultmann called "demythologization." As an approach, psychobiography attempts to demythologize lives that are challenging to interpret, especially ones that are knotty with contradictions, shifting centers of meaning, moral ambiguities, and apocryphal narratives. Of course, comprehensive biographies like Clinton Heylin's *Behind the Shades* are after a similar end. But psychobiography differs from biography in terms of focus. It attempts to capture the unique psychological "fingerprint" of a person by trying to make sense of an idiosyncratic, hard-to-pin-down part of him or her that contributes significantly to identity and behavior. The personality psychologist

Henry Murray once wrote that we are all in some respects like all other people, like some other people, and like no other people (Murray & Kluckhohn, 1953). Psychobiography tackles this last piece, the part of a person that's unique and that may resist easy intelligibility. It asks *why* someone is the way he or she is—then draws on psychological theory and experimental research to address the question. Much like the hagiographical tradition of the Middle Ages, psychobiography is after the essence of lives. The two genres are similar insofar as they concern themselves with a specific feature or virtue within the lives of their subjects, whether it's Saint Francis's relationship to the natural world or Jack Kerouac's lifelong search for his dead brother, Gerard. This sort of approach is at odds with the "who knows more" scholasticism of Dylan studies, where Dylanologists battle over the dating of songs, the names of girlfriends, and the exact number of children he has had outside of his two known marriages. The field of Dylanology, consequently, has reached a point of absurdity. To quote from Dylan's 2006 song "Nettie Moore," on the album *Modern Times*, "The world of research has gone berserk / too much paper work." Psychobiography tries to cut through the biographical paper work with one or more claims about a person's underlying motivations prompted by a well-crafted psychological question.

Beyond being one of the most lauded and loved songwriters and performers of all time, there are multiple other reasons why Dylan's life is worth thinking about. First of all, there is much to be learned in the study of cultural icons. Such individuals come to symbolize many of our shared fantasies and fears as a society. In 1985, *Spin Magazine* asked Dylan if there was anyone that he would enjoy interviewing himself. Dylan's response: Hank Williams, Apollinaire, Marilyn Monroe, John F. Kennedy, Joseph of Arimathea, Mohammed, and Paul the Apostle. He is then quoted saying, "I'd like to interview people who died leaving a great unsolved mess behind, who left people for ages to do nothing but speculate." During my doctoral years, I heard the adage *to understand one person is to understand the world.* This strikes me as especially true of iconic lives. An understanding of why Norma Jean changed her appearance and became Marilyn Monroe—or why Hank Williams wrote the music that he did—paint human portraits that teach us a good deal about the times, places, and circumstances that helped create these individuals, in addition to the roles their lives play in the constructions of our own identities.

Second, we live in an age dominated by pathography, a term that refers to biographies that reduce subjects to unresolved conflicts, limitations, and hang-ups. Explaining Simone Weil's attraction to ascetic spirituality as a consequence of her lifelong struggle with an eating disorder or Leonardo da Vinci's Mona Lisa as a symptom of underlying sexual ambivalence (as Freud once did) offers a simplistic interpretation of complex phenomena. Claiming that someone is bipolar, clinically depressed, or bulimic may help make sense of a range of behaviors, but such labels do little to advance an understanding of personality. The particulars of a life should be consulted for that sort of understanding, not the *Diagnostic Statistical Manual of Mental Disorders* (DSM). The diagnostic categories in the DSM replace the dynamics of personality with a homogenizing checklist of symptoms. There are no etiological speculations and no case studies in this compendium of mental diseases, currently in its fifth iteration. Personality *cannot* be winnowed down to a facile equation or cliché. Personality is bigger than clichés. To quote from Walt Whitman's *Song of Myself,* "I am large . . . I contain multitudes."

There is clear merit to studying lives that are generative. The French existential philosopher Jean Paul Sartre characterized the proper study of a man as determining "what he succeeds in making of what he has been made." Living a generative life involves going beyond the immediate biological and social needs of one's existence and creating *something shining* (e.g., a body of work or legacy) that engenders purpose and benefits future generations. People who score highly on indicators of generativity teach us about the utmost potentials of human life and development, demonstrating the various shapes that a life can take. Ever since the pioneering work of William James, academic psychology has examined the extent to which adult personality can be reconfigured beyond genetic and environmental constraints. The lives of people who are particularly generative offer valuable insights into both the plasticity and deterministic limitations of who we are as a species. A fascinating part of Bob Dylan's generativity involves the myriad changes that he has experienced as an artist. The more striking of these turns in the road coincide with transformations at the levels of identity and personality.

The six chapters that follow offer a modest glimpse into the inner life of Bob Dylan, who, in case you're wondering, I've never met. When I finally tracked down someone who claimed to have access to him, I was told that Mr. Dylan wasn't interested in speaking about his thoughts and feelings and generally gave only one high-profile interview (e.g., with *60 Minutes, Rolling Stone,* etc.) per major project. Even if I had been granted an audience, it's unlikely that he'd have a clear picture of his own motives because people almost never do. Thankfully, the absence of direct access to a subject doesn't prevent good psychobiography from being done. Enough documentary evidence, in addition to a mixture of critical judgment, historical perspective, and a willingness to discern order from disorder are the most vital ingredients. And at the heart of it all must be an ethical commitment not to exploit or sensationalize the subject. Rembrandt's portraits and Leonardo da Vinci's anatomical drawings are better models for life studies than the salacious "tell-all's" that dominate the popular biographical marketplace.

During the process of drafting this book, I was asked what was new about my take on Dylan. But the task of a good psychobiographer or any researcher doing qualitative work on a life isn't to generate a new theory. Striving for originality for its own sake runs the risk of producing a caricature. The goal, rather, is to construct a representative portrait of a person as he or she experiences and understands his or her life. The narrative psychologist and artist Suzanne Ouellette has written on how the psychological study of a person and portrait painting share similarities. Ouellette writes, "As I paint, I seek to recognize and look through prior social constructions to capture in paint the reality I see in my distinctive way; a way that represents both the individuality of the person I am painting, and a few small truths about what it means to be a person that strike me as transcending the particular individual in a particular pose." The same can be said of good psychobiography. Such portraits aim to capture "not the lifetime of one man only / But of old stones that cannot be deciphered," as T. S. Eliot puts it in *Four Quartets*.

This work requires the delicate art of bringing a life into form and faithfully accenting its surfaces with color. Bob Dylan, of course, is notorious for refusing to sit still for long. He is a prince of protean self-reinvention and deflection. His wheeling, dealing, and jiving during interviews have led to a dizzying accumulation of masks. But I hope to show how a careful look across the surfaces of these masks reveals the depths of a life characterized by more unity than disunity, more coherence than fragmentation. And at the heart of this coherence is a repetitive story of spiritual death and rebirth grounded in a sonic mystery religion that Bob Dylan first heard as kid in the Forties by turning the dial of the family radio.

It bears mentioning from the outset that I'm not trying to explain why Dylan composed the songs and lyrics that he did. In a letter to Carl Jung, Freud wrote, "Before the problem of the creative artist analysis must, alas, lay down its arms." Believing that human beings were "over-determined," he was doubtful that psychoanalysis could penetrate the sources of creativity, writing elsewhere that "all genuinely creative writings are the products of more than a single motive and more than a single impulse in the poet's mind, and are open to more than a single interpretation." I agree with this assessment. What this book does do is to search Dylan's self-descriptions and some lyrics for recurring themes and plotlines that help make psychological sense of his many personal and artistic changes over the decades.

LIGHT COME SHINING

1 | MASKED AND ANONYMOUS

Man is a "choice," a struggle, a constant becoming. He is an
infinite migration, a migration within himself, from clay to
God; he is a migrant within his own soul.

—Ali Shariati

Bob Dylan's transformations from his early days on the folk
scene in New York City to the present have been an object
of fascination to the point of cliché and parody. He has been
called the man who wasn't there, a complete unknown, a mystery
tramp, to name only a few of many monikers. The Russian philosopher Mikhail Bakhtin conceived of people as "unfinalizable,"
as constantly in a state of becoming. According to this view, we're
continually changing, and no person can ever be fully known by
others—or by oneself for that matter. This process view of being
human fits Bob Dylan like a glove. "Nothing stays where it is for
very long," he said to Mikal Gilmore in 2012. "Trees grow tall,
leaves fall, rivers dry up and flowers die. New people are born
every day. Life doesn't stop." Similarly, in Martin Scorsese's documentary *No Direction Home* (2005), Dylan explains that, as an
artist, he can't ever feel as if he has "arrived somewhere" and that
he has to "be constantly in a state of becoming." The wiry, wild-
haired mid-Sixties poet/prophet with his sunglasses and acoustic

guitar was only one in a series of colorful personae through which Dylan has morphed over the years. It has been frustrating to him that who he was during those days has become a fixture of his legend. He has referred to himself as someone who spends each day living in the ruins of Pompeii. Everywhere he goes, he encounters images of who he was at a much earlier moment in his life, even though the wizened Delta blues–obsessed troubadour he has become bears only a minimal resemblance to the "Bob Dylan" that many concertgoers pay money hoping to see. Although he can still pull off a spirited live performance, online and print reviews of his shows are rife with disappointed commentary on how his look and sound have changed. A 2012 concert review that appeared in the *Toronto Star* reflected on how Dylan cleared out the sparsely attended arena by "bloody mindedly playing the crank and serving up an uncompromising mix of rambling recent numbers rendered in the jump-blues vein and thoroughly (read: almost unrecognizably) worked-over catalogue standards such as 'A Hard Rain's a-Gonna Fall,' 'Blind Willie McTell,' and a set-concluding grind on 'Blowin' in the Wind.'"

Perusing the sizable library of published materials on his life and work reveals much more than appraisals of his stunning catalogue of music. They participate in a fifty-plus-year attempt to find the man amid the twists and turns of a rock-n-roll legend. The titles of popular Dylan biographies and documentaries reveal the celebrity cult that has trailed him since his twenties. *Behind the Shades, Who Is That Man?: In Search of the Real Bob Dylan, Alias Bob Dylan Revisited, Bob Dylan Revealed*, and *The Other Side of the Mirror* dangle the mystery of who Dylan *really* is, promising a portrait of the man stripped of his myriad masks. But in the words of filmmaker Todd Haynes, who cast six actors to depict different facets of Dylan's life and artistic personae in his 2009 film *I'm Not There*: "The minute you try to grab hold of Dylan, he's no longer where he was. He's like a flame: If you try to hold him in your hand you'll surely get burned. Dylan's life of change and constant disappearances and constant transformations makes you yearn to hold him, and to nail him down."

Even Dylan's physical appearance has been couched in terms of changeability. According to friend and fellow early-1960s folk singer Eric von Schmidt, Dylan had "the most incredible way of changing shape, changing size, changing looks. The whole time . . . he wore the same thing, his blue jeans and cap. And sometimes he would look big and muscular, and the next day he'd look like a little gnome, and one day he'd be kind of handsome and virile, and the following day he'd look like a thirteen-year-old child" (quoted in Cott, 2006, x).

His style of singing over the years is another moving target. The same voice that was described by Minnesotan friends as "pretty" and "beautiful" in his late teens transformed into the nasally timbre immortalized on classic albums from the mid-1960s, like *Highway 61 Revisited* (1965) and *Blonde on Blonde* (1966). His voice then evolved into the Bing Crosby croon of *Nashville Skyline* (1969) and *Self-Portrait* (1970). The lungful power of his vocal work during the mid-Seventies ascended into the prayerful precision of his gospel period. Gradually, over the decades, the quality of his voice has lowered and narrowed in range into the gravelly lilt that has characterized his singing in recent years.

With no small degree of irony, Bob Dylan began having his road manager introduce him before every live show starting in August 2002 with an announcement parodying his more recognizable changes:

Ladies and gentleman please welcome the poet laureate of rock-n-roll. The voice of the promise of the '60s counterculture. The guy who forced folk into bed with rock. Who donned makeup in the '70s and disappeared into a haze of substance abuse. Who emerged to find Jesus. Who was written off as a has-been by the end of the '80s, and who suddenly shifted gears releasing some of the strongest music of his career beginning in the late '90s. Ladies and gentleman— Columbia recording artist Bob Dylan![1]

In a similar spirit, Robert Shelton chose to begin his fawning biography, *No Direction Home: The Life and Music of Bob Dylan* (2010), with a sentence that capitalized on the theme of death and rebirth: "This is a story about a poet and musician who was born and reborn time again, who 'died' several 'deaths' and yet continued to live" (Shelton, 2010, 13). This mercurial quality is intriguing to say the least. But people change over a lifetime, some in striking ways; Bob Dylan is hardly unique in this respect. Erik Erikson (1968) believed that it wasn't unusual for creative people to reexamine and renegotiate their identities more often and intensely than other people. The artistic careers of David Bowie, Madonna,

1. This introduction was adapted from an article by Jeff Miers that appeared in *The Buffalo News* on August 9, 2002.

and Lady Gaga, for example, are all marked by change over time. Yet, for Dylan, unlike for Bowie or the others, the changes suggest transformations at the level of personality. Alongside his musical changes, it wasn't uncommon for Dylan to change his spoken vernacular, his ideas about spirituality, the company he kept, and the self-defining memories that he shared during interviews. Dylan, who referred to himself in 2012 as a *transfigured* person, has frequently made reference to a feeling of *personal destiny* behind the constant becoming that has shaped his life.

Why did he leave Minneapolis for New York City with no clear plan or regular place to stay? Why did he change his name from Robert Zimmerman to Bob Dylan? Why did he disappear from the public eye for several years at the peak of his fame? Why did he convert to Christianity and attempt to evangelize the audiences who paid to see him play? Why did he recommit himself to singing and songwriting after nearly quitting the music business in the late Eighties? His answer: It was *destiny*. This powerful force compelled him to keep moving on, turning corners, disappearing, reappearing—changing his voice, image, and musical style. It's not simply an evasive way of deflecting the inquiries of journalists in search of rational explanations to nonrational experiences. Nor is it the slippery performance of a trickster or confidence man worthy of Herman Melville or Mark Twain. It's a piece of poetry used by Dylan to explain a defining feature of his inner life.

In this book, I argue that the best place to find Dylan's unique psychological fingerprint is within the twists and turns of his changes. Furthermore, I show how his autobiographical reflections on the more significant of these changes reveal a recurring narrative (a *script*) that can be traced back to his childhood growing up in the Iron Range of northern Minnesota. This script suggests the presence of an abiding psychological structure that has driven Dylan's transformations over the years. In particular, the script undergirds three major turning points, all of which he has couched in terms of personal destiny: the aftermath of his 1966 motorcycle "accident," his Born Again conversion experience in 1978, and his recommitment to songwriting and performing in 1987. Across all three episodes, destiny manifested itself, and Dylan felt that he had no choice but to follow its drums.

Ever since William James proposed that personality was set in plaster (1890/1950), psychology has explored whether or not personality can change dramatically over the life span. Developmental psychologists like Erikson (1959) disagreed with James and argued for change across a series of psychosocial stages from infancy through old age. Likewise, psychoanalytic and clinical traditions have placed positive change at the center of the therapeutic process. Personality psychologists such as Dan McAdams and Jennifer Pals (2006), however, have drawn on extensive empirical research to contend that individuals remain relatively constant at the level of dispositional traits but malleable at other levels. They conceptualize personality as five interrelated levels—an individual's unique variation on the evolutionary design for human nature expressed as a pattern of dispositional traits, characteristic adaptations, and self-defining narratives situated in specific sociocultural contexts. According to the authors' vast survey of research, characteristic adaptions and life narratives are the most likely to show considerable change over time. So, in addition to biological and psychosocial changes accompanying developmental maturation, people can alter their cognitive/affective responses as well as the personal stories they tell to themselves and others about who they are.

Personality change can look more dramatic, too. Even James, despite suggesting that personality was "set in plaster" by the age of thirty (1890), wrote about sudden conversion experiences in *The Varieties of Religious Experience* (1902).[2] He characterized these transformational experiences as leading to sudden, dramatic shifts in the "habitual center" of "personal energy." James traced out a familiar conversion script in which "a sudden flood" of emotional energy altered the ideas and values at the center of one's identity. James noticed that subjects would frequently appeal to a spiritual language when explaining what they'd been through. The personal stories he examined cited God's plan and divine grace in particular. In more recent decades, William Miller and Janet C'deBaca of the University of New Mexico have continued James's work on fundamental change.[3] Referred to by the authors as *quantum change*, this curious phenomenon has been documented in response to spiritual/religious transformations, after seismic shifts in career or occupation, and during recovery from traumatic events.

The transformations described by the participants studied by Miller and C'deBaca are marked by four common qualities: (1) the magnitude and sudden onset of the experience, (2) being

2. In *The Varieties*, James made note of two types of religious conversion: a willful or *volitional type* and a more sudden and affective type called the *type by self-surrender*.
3. Miller, William R., & C'deBaca, Janet. (2001). *Quantum Change: When Epiphanies and Sudden Insights Transform Ordinary Lives*. New York: Guilford Press.

markedly different from ordinary change, (3) involving pervasive change across identity and behavior, and (4) enduring over time. Many "quantum changers" claim that some external agent or force prompted their changes, which often come "out of nowhere" and which were challenging to explain. As James (1902) once said of mystical phenomena, such experiences possess a character of ineffability.

The majority of the subjects interviewed by Miller and C'deBaca trace their transformational experiences back to specific turning points or scenes. These episodes often become defining memories for the individuals who undergo them and are narrated with great care and detail for years and decades into the future—eventually becoming what narrative researchers call "self-defining" memories (e.g., Singer and Bagov, 2004). Bob Dylan has characterized his changes in a language reminiscent of Miller and C'deBaca's subjects, especially those who describe the change as a spiritual awakening and experience of transcendence that liberates them from negative circumstances by creating an altered and redemptive inner picture of the self.

Despite a reputation for manipulating the media, Dylan has tried to describe his major turning points in great detail over the years. According to Clinton Heylin, there are periods in his career when he has discussed his life with candor and depth. For instance, the years 1978 and 1985 house some of Dylan's more forthcoming exchanges with the press. The same can be said for his 2004 memoir *Chronicles: Volume One*, which, despite its apocryphal anecdotes and novelistic structure, may have been an attempt on Dylan's part to set the record straight about his past. Across the following chapters, I will offer content analyses of the interviews and autobiographical writings in which he discusses the turning points mentioned earlier. In order to provide some context, though, it's important first to sketch an outline of Bob Dylan's "public" biography as it stands after fifty years of investigation.

The Bob Dylan Legend

Bob Dylan was born Robert Zimmerman in 1941, into a comfortable middle-class Jewish household in Duluth, Minnesota, although he grew up in the northern mining town of Hibbing. The mining companies had extracted all the available ore from the land, so jobs weren't as plentiful as they once were. Dylan reports an early awareness of the region's ecological and economic struggles. He was also aware of the Cold War tensions with the Soviet Union and felt the threat of a nuclear attack from the age of ten onward. This general anxiety was assuaged some by the emotional and material support of his parents. Beatty, his mother, was the dotting guardian of her two little boys, Bob and his younger brother David.[4] His father, Abraham, was distant and hardworking, though by most accounts a dedicated family man who provided handsomely for his wife and two sons, who he expected to live by his code of honesty, family, and hard work. Dylan and Abe would never have a particularly close relationship, however. Abe was the son of Jewish immigrants from Odessa who'd fled

4. David has refrained from saying much on the record about his older brother ever since speaking candidly to *Newsweek Magazine* in 1963 and deeply hurting and angering Dylan.

a pogrom, and Beatty came from a family of Lithuanian Jews that immigrated to Minnesota the same decade as her husband's family. Stricken by polio shortly after his younger son's birth and unable to continue working for his employer, Standard Oil, Abe's dreams of advancement within the company and a life with his family in Duluth were dashed. With Beatty's encouragement, he moved his family to his wife's hometown of Hibbing, where he worked his way up in a hardware and appliance store owned by two of his brothers. Between Hibbing and Duluth, Bob and David grew up in a close-knit northern Jewish community of relatives and friends.

Dylan describes his childhood as restless in *Chronicles*: "It seemed I'd always been chasing after something, anything that moved—a car, a bird, a blowing leaf—anything that might lead me into some more lit place, some unknown land downriver." And that river was none other than the mighty Mississippi, which runs from northern Minnesota straight on down to the Delta. "The Mississippi River, the bloodstream of the blues, also starts up from my neck of the woods. I was never too far away from any of it. It was my place in the universe, always felt like it was in my blood" (Dylan, 2004, 241).

Another line of travel that entranced him was the literal and figurative Highway 61, "the main thoroughfare of the blues." Dylan writes, "I always felt like I'd started on it, always had been on it and could go anywhere from it, even down into the deep Delta country" (Dylan, 2004, 240). Enamored by Delta blues, country, early rock-n-roll, and Big Band music he heard over the AM radio, he picked up piano, then guitar, and played in a handful of amplified garage bands. As a teenager, he rode a motorbike around, wore a leather jacket in the style of James Dean from *A Rebel Without a Cause*, and used his swagger to woo a handful of local girls. Although Abe provided his wayward son with an allowance and financed the motorbike and various pieces of musical equipment, the two didn't see eye to eye and were frequently at odds. Dylan writes about their tensions candidly in *Chronicles*: "Growing up, the cultural and generational differences had been insurmountable—nothing but the sound of voices, colorless unnatural speech. . . . The town he lived in and the town I lived in were not the same" (Dylan, 2004, 107–108).

In 1959, he delighted his worried parents by heading off to the University of Minnesota, in Minneapolis. He moved in with a cousin who resided at the university's Jewish fraternity house. But he soon abandoned the buttoned-up world of academics for the folk and beat poetry scene around Minneapolis's bohemian enclave, Dinkytown. It was there that he fell under the enchanting influence of Woody Guthrie's music and loosely spun autobiography *Bound for Glory,* which quickly surpassed Kerouac's *On the Road* as his cultural fulcrum. Before long, he became an aficionado of folk songs. With the help of folksinger friends like John Koerner, he began working up a repertoire of traditional ballads and talking blues that he soon performed at clubs like The Purple Onion and The Ten O'clock Scholar.

The winter after an influential summer honing his craft in and around Denver, he cut his ties to the university and made his way to New York City to meet his hero, Guthrie, who was suffering from Huntington's chorea and living at a state hospital in Morristown, New Jersey. Despite their misgivings, Abe and Beatty decided to fund their son for one year during his musical adventures in "New York Town," with the agreement that he'd return to his studies if his musical aspirations failed to pan out.

It wasn't long before the Chaplinesque twenty-year-old took the Greenwich Village folk community by storm. Described as a human sponge, he absorbed everything he possibly could from established players on the scene like Dave Van Ronk, Richie Havens, and Ramblin' Jack Elliott, and he played a two-week residency at Gerde's Folk City, opening up for the blues great John Lee Hooker within a year of his arrival. Shortly after being praised by Robert Shelton in the *New York Times* in September 1961 as "a bright new face in folk music . . . bursting at the seams with talent," Dylan was offered a coveted recording contract with Columbia Records by the legendary John Hammond. As his reputation as a major talent increased, so did the imaginative scope of his personal narrative, which established early on that knowing the dancer from the dance would be challenging. "If you told the truth, that was all well and good and if you told the un-truth, well, that's still well and good," Dylan would write decades later. "Folk songs had taught me that."

The more that people inquired, the more fantastical his yarns became. His August 1962 decision to legally change his name from Robert Allen Zimmerman to Bob Dylan was only one of a growing number of experiments in the arena of identity. Like many of the colorful personalities who hung around Greenwich Village, Dylan played out the role of an improvisational character spun together from a shifting constellation of Steinbeck, Beat novels, folklore, and, above all else, Woody Guthrie's *Bound for Glory*. He told a bunch of people that he was an orphan from New Mexico, part Sioux Indian and part Irish-English-Welsh-Okie. He falsely claimed that when he wasn't running away from the orphanage as a child, he was bounced between foster families. One of these families included a riverboat gambling uncle and another uncle who was a professional burglar. It wasn't long before he ran away from there as well, or so he said. Joining a traveling carnival at the age of thirteen, he supposedly worked greasing the Ferris wheel and driving tent stakes. He purportedly crisscrossed the South and Southwest playing piano for the carnival dancers. While in New Mexico, an old man named Wigglefoot with a patch and missing teeth taught him how to play the bottleneck slide guitar. After his carnival days were through, he found work grooming horses and shoveling manure on a ranch. Then, at some point later he allegedly operated a steam shovel and forklift up and down the mining country from northern Minnesota clear on down to the Texas–Mexico border. Giving into his wanderlust completely, he hopped freight trains and hung out with hobos, growing his hair and nails long and doing nothing but drinking jug wine and picking on his guitar.

The exaggerations and lies kept piling up. During a stint in Texas, he claimed meeting the sharecropping Delta bluesman Black Mance Lipscomb and learning the older man's style and repertoire. Dylan then claimed traveling to Detroit, Chicago, and Denver, playing for anyone who'd listen, picking up musical tips from players in the clubs and on the curbs. There was a short sojourn in Minnesota as a piano player in Bobby Vee's Band, which was partially true, and a mythical trip to California to see Woody Guthrie perform in Carmel, California, with Ramblin' Jack Elliott and Billy Faier, which was patently false. Sometime later, he heard Woody was sick in a state hospital around New York and hopped a freight train east to visit his hero, arriving on a blusteringly cold and snowy day in January 1961 amidst two feet of snow.

In an interview with Robert Shelton, Dylan even concocted a story of working as a male hustler around Time Square for a spell before making his way downtown. "I shucked everybody when I came to New York," he is quoted as saying. "I played cute. I did not go down to the Village when I first got to New York. I have a friend . . . he's a junkie now. We came to New York together. He wrote plays. We hung out on 43rd Street, and hustled for two months, and did everything. I got the ride here in December 1960. I came down to the Village in February. But I was here, in New York, in December. Hustling, with this cat." Shelton apparently believed the story because he included it in his biography.

In addition to elevating its celebrities and public officials into demigods, there's nothing the American media enjoys more than tearing them down. A stinging 1963 *Newsweek* article written by reporter Andrea Svedburg exposed that, despite his claims of being a train-hopping Oakie, Bob Dylan was born Robert Zimmerman into a comfortable household in Duluth, Minnesota, and raised in Hibbing, where his father, Abe Zimmerman, ran a family-owned appliance and furniture store and his mother, Beatty, kept a comfortable and nurturing household. The article also revealed that Dylan changed his name legally on August 9, 1962, and hurtfully concluded: "Why Dylan—he picked the name in admiration for Dylan Thomas—should bother to deny his past is a mystery. Perhaps he feels it would spoil the image he works so hard to cultivate. . . . There is even a rumor circulating that Dylan did not write 'Blowin' in the Wind.' . . . Dylan says he is writing a book that will explain everything. But, he insists, the explanations are irrelevant. 'I am my words', he says." This instance would be the first of a near-constant stream of articles, exposes, and unauthorized biographies to probe, dissect, and interrogate his private life, the pressure of which would turn him over time into a paranoid recluse whose attempts to safeguard his own privacy amounted to an increasingly eccentric lifestyle.

The *Newsweek* article purportedly threw a young Dylan into a lengthy depression, but it also added complexity to his mystique, which, in turn, benefited his career in no small measure. Those who stood to benefit from his fame socially and financially took immediate notice. The forceful and farsighted manager Albert Grossman began representing him in 1962. In *Chronicles*, Dylan describes his first impressions of Grossman at the Gaslight Café: "He looked like Sydney Greenstreet from the film *The Maltese Falcon*, had an enormous presence, always dressed in a conventional suit and tie, and he sat at his corner table. Usually when he talked, his voice was loud like the booming of war drums. He didn't talk so much as growl" (Dylan, 2004). Grossman, who managed acts such as Peter, Paul and Mary, The Band, Odetta, and Janis Joplin over his career, knew it was possible to capitalize on both Dylan's musical genius and his unpredictable persona. Whether to record labels, network television, or publishing companies, he was willing to sell the Dylan brand to any person or organization with coffers big enough to afford his sizable fees, which ended up making both Dylan and himself millionaires in a relatively short period of time.

The popularity of "Blowin' in the Wind" and "The Times They Are a-Changin'" catapulted Dylan into the national spotlight within two years of being signed to Columbia. Chronically restless, however, he couldn't sit still for long and resented being treated like "a trained seal." He was championed by an adoring Joan Baez (with whom he was romantically involved) but dropped her during his meteoric rise to international stardom. By the mid-Sixties, he'd eschewed protest songs for surrealistic and paradoxical themes that were anything but topical, razzing folk purists like Pete Seeger and Allan Lomax with his infamous full-throttle three-song electric set at the 1965 Newport Folk Festival. After recording some of the most influential rock music of all time across 1965 and 1966 with *Highway 61 Revisited* and *Blonde on Blonde*, he embarked upon a turbulent drug-fueled world tour. The pace and intensity pushed the limits of his audiences as well as his own mind and body to the point of collapse, culminating in a mysterious motorcycle accident on a rural road outside Woodstock, New York. Although the physical accident was likely a put-on to allow him space and time to slow down and recalibrate, the state of his consciousness and extent of his physical exhaustion were serious health matters. Looking back in 2012, he'd refer to the accident as having led to a "transfiguration," which is typically thought of as a Catholic theological term that involves a change of form or appearance into a more realized spiritual state.

After the accident came a period of self-imposed withdrawal to rest and raise a family with his first wife Sara Lownds, whom Dylan secretly married several months earlier and with whom he'd father four children: Jesse, Anna, Samuel, and Jakob. Dylan also adopted Maria, Lownds's daughter from her first marriage to the magazine fashion photographer Hans Lownds. During this reclusive period, he recorded the *Basement Tapes* with The Band in Saugerties, New York, and a cluster of country albums in Nashville and New York City. Gradually, he resumed playing the occasional concert, beginning with a Woody Guthrie benefit in 1968, one year after his idol's death from Huntington's chorea.

In the early Seventies, Dylan released a series of commercial flops (e.g., the double length *Self Portrait* and *New Morning*), which he now claims were a way of sabotaging the "legend" status that trailed him everywhere he went, interrupting and fragmenting his life. But after his attempts at anonymity proved futile and his domestic life began to strain and drag, Dylan "faced the music" by hitting the road on a debauching stadium world tour with The Band in 1974. The years that followed found Dylan living between New York, a farm in Minnesota, and Monterrey, California. He recorded and released the critically well-received albums *Blood on the Tracks* and *Desire*, and embarked on a carnival-style Commedia dell'arte tour of small northeastern theaters and larger southern venues with a troupe of homespun musicians, poets, and performers called Rolling Thunder Revue. On the heels of the tour, Dylan edited and released a critically lampooned four-hour film called *Renaldo and Clara* that featured footage from the Revue juxtaposed with improvised scenes. The flop of *Renaldo and Clara* was especially painful because Dylan thought of the movie as the most personally meaningful piece of art he'd ever produced.

In 1978, Dylan and Sara divorced acrimoniously after struggling for several years. In addition to her husband's rampant womanizing and a jarring incident of physical violence, Sara feared for the safety of her children who, she claimed, were greatly disturbed by her husband's behavior and bizarre lifestyle. After a Big Band Vegas-style world tour that some critics dubbed the "alimony tour," a road-weary Dylan underwent his second major "transfiguration," a full-blown Born Again Christian conversion that inspired the recording of a trilogy of gospel albums: *Slow Train Coming* (1979), *Saved* (1980), and *Shot of Love* (1981). He began traveling around more regularly with a trio of Black female backup singers (a.k.a. the Queens of Rhythm) and for a time refused to play any of his pre-Christian music. A previously shy Dylan openly preached to audiences with mini-sermons between songs, saying things like—"Anyway, we know this world's gonna be destroyed; we know that. Christ will set up His Kingdom in Jerusalem for a thousand years, where the lion will lie down with the lamb. Have you heard that before? I'm just curious enough to know, how many people believe that?" Many of his fans never forgave him. But he was adamant about evangelizing, at least for a while. From his perspective, the end of the world was nigh, and the only option was to repent and be saved. The alternative was eternal damnation in the fiery pit of hell.

The Eighties witnessed a mellowing of his religious rhetoric; a second marriage to a backup singer named Carolyn Dennis, with whom he fathered his sixth child, Desiree (b. 1986); a string of slipshod albums (*Empire Burlesque, Knocked Out Loaded*, and *Down in the Groove* come to mind); and several embarrassing public missteps. For example, he delivered a humiliatingly shaky performance with a visibly intoxicated Keith Richards and Ron Wood of The Rolling Stones to a television audience estimated at 1 billion at Live Aid in 1985. According to reports, he was drinking copiously and feeling thoroughly uninspired. After he seriously considered giving up music in the late 1980s, Dylan experienced his third major turning point in a bar in San Rafael, during rehearsals with the Grateful Dead in 1987. This experience, which has mystical overtones reminiscent of his conversion experience a decade earlier, impelled Dylan to recommit himself to his craft. Feeling more certain of his destiny, he returned to American musical roots and recorded two critically acclaimed albums of traditional cover songs in the early Nineties called *Good As I Been to You* and *World Gone Wrong*. But it was the Grammy-winning album *Time Out of Mind* in 1997 and chart-topping *Love and Theft* in 2001 that reinvigorated his career in later midlife, fueling his so-called never-ending tour, in motion since 1988, with critical acclaim and a widening demographic of old and new fans.

Since 2001, Dylan has released a cluster of studio albums, a treasure-trove of rare and unreleased bootleg recordings, and two collections of cover songs—*Christmas in the Heart* (2009) and *Shadows in the Night* (2015), a collection of songs recorded, sung, and popularized by one of Dylan's heroes, Frank Sinatra. His live shows (upward of one hundred per year), though, remain his primary focus as an artist. He tours every year from the early spring until November and spends his months off the road with his family. He claims rarely listening to his albums once they're done and thinks of them as snapshots of the real thing, which can only occur on stage. After a peak in live performance around the early millennium, the quality of his shows has become maddeningly unpredictable. In recent years, perhaps because of arthritic hands, Dylan has alternated between the guitar, organ, piano, or singing without playing an accompanying instrument. His voice croons, barks, and lilts over a backdrop of blaringly amplified honky-tonk and bluesy rock skillfully played by an adept band of world-class musicians.

The blood of the land that pulses through Dylan's voice isn't pretty to listen to, but neither were the gravelly tones of his Delta blues heroes like Charley Patton or Howlin' Wolf. He was booed for selling out in his twenties, scrutinized for finding Jesus in his late thirties, and he's now written off as a has-been for the cardinal sin of getting old. Regardless of how uneven some find his performances, the fan consensus seems to be that each show promises at least one transcendent moment, whether a rawboned "Simple Twist of Fate," a longingly dejected version of "Forgetful Heart," or a shadowy rendition of "Not Dark Yet" worthy of Dante's *Inferno*. The lines from "Tangled Up in Blue," "But me I'm still on the road / Heading for another joint," have never been more true. Thus, it's hard for Dylan fans to imagine the day when he'll be gone, transfigured completely into his songs.

The Bob Dylan Mask

Nietzsche once wrote that, "Every profound spirit needs a mask: even more, around every profound spirit a mask is growing continually, owing to the constantly false, namely shallow, interpretation of every word, every step, every sign of life he gives." Dylan has long been frustrated by the shallow and erroneous interpretations that swirl around him. "The press has always misrepresented me," he said in an interview during the mid-Seventies. "They refuse to accept what I am and what I do. They always sensationalize and blow things up. . . . It makes me feel better to write one song than talk to a thousand journalists." Some forty years later, in 2015, he'd express a similar sentiment when reflecting on the history of his critical reception: "Well you know, I just thought I was doing something natural, but right from the start, my songs were divisive for some reason. They divided people. I never knew why. Some got angered, others loved them. Didn't know why my songs had detractors and supporters. A strange environment to have to throw your songs into, but I did it anyway."

Given this mistrust of journalists, his desire for privacy has made him paranoid and cantankerous over the years. He told Allen Ginsberg that fame was a burden with no redeeming qualities, and he has expressed everything from ambivalence to disdain for unsolicited interactions with fans and admirers. Such interactions constitute "dead time" from his perspective. He refrains from going out to eat in public and even took to wearing a spooky blond wig and skullcap when out. And he believes that the emotional connection many fans feel to him is an illusion of the performance that has little to do with who he is. "To me, the relationship between performer and audience is anything but a buddy-buddy thing, any more than me going in and admiring a Van Gogh painting and thinking me and him are on the same level," he told Jann Wenner in 2007. Aside from a small number of carefully selected interviews promoting specific projects, Dylan avoids journalists and biographers.

Still, the media's relentless scrutiny seems to have taken a toll on the aging legend. "Why is it that when people talk about me they have to go crazy? What the fuck is the matter with them?" Dylan asked Mikal Gilmore in the same 2012 interview in which he referred to himself as transfigured. "Sure, I played with the Band. Yeah, I made a record called *John Wesley Harding*. And sure, I sounded different. So fucking what? They want to know what can't be known. . . . Why are they doing this? They don't really know. It's sad. It really is. May the Lord have mercy on them. They are lost souls. They really don't know. It's sad—it really is. It's sad for me, and it's sad for them." Eleven years earlier, Dylan expressed similar contempt for the burgeoning field of Dylanology: "These so-called connoisseurs of Bob Dylan music . . . I don't feel they know a thing, or have any inkling of who I am or what I'm about. I know they think they do, and yet it's ludicrous, it's humorous, and sad. That such people have spent too much of their time thinking about who? Me? Get a life, please. It's not something any one person should do about another. You're not serving your own life well. You're wasting your life."

This playful and at times antagonistic relationship with the press dates back to his early years on the folk scene in New York. When asked about his identity by straight-laced reporters with buzz cuts and sport coats, he frequently answered sarcastically: "a trapeze artist," "a song and dance man," "an ashtray bender," and "a rabbit catcher." Some of the more memorable moments from D. A. Pennebaker's 1967 documentary *Dont Look Back*, which chronicles Dylan's 1965 tour of England, involve Q&A sessions with reporters that elicit responses that range from absurdist to downright hostile. Dylan, ever-performing for Pennebaker's camera, comes across as a bratty hipster. An entourage surrounds him at all times like a hive of spastic bees. His dark sunglasses, unruly hair, incessant cigarette smoking, and spitfire verbosity present the portrait of an amphetamine-fed young virtuoso trying to manage his considerable talent and fame. One stratagem was to lie to the press. Dylan explains during one interview that journalists were to be toyed with or ignored. "They ask the wrong questions," he said, "like, What did you have for breakfast, What's your favorite color, stuff like that. Newspaper reporters, man, they're just hung up writers. . . . They got all these preconceived ideas about me, so I just play up to them." The sardonic lyrics to his classic 1965 song "Ballad of a Thin Man" reflect the reality of an artist actively resisting the reductionisms of a journalist infamously named Mister Jones. The memorable first verse goes:

> You walk into the room
> With your pencil in your hand
> You see somebody naked
> And you say, "Who is that man?"
> You try so hard
> But you don't understand
> Just what you'll say
> When you get home

In *Chronicles*, Dylan writes about the public theater he engaged in to throw off the paparazzi, journalists, and fans who kept him from settling into a normal life after his retreat from the limelight in Woodstock. He traveled to Jerusalem and got himself photographed at the Western Wall wearing a skullcap, and he leaked a story to the press that he planned to give up songwriting altogether and attend the Rhode Island School of Design. He was besieged by sensational stories published by people he'd never met. Some claimed that he was on an eternal search for meaning or in great inner torment. "The press?" Dylan writes in his memoir. "I figured you lie to it. For the public eye, I went into the bucolic and mundane as far as possible" (Dylan, 2004, 123). He was trying to protect his wife and children from the intrusions of celebrity, not to mention his sense of sanity. And compared to others artists who were quite literally killed by it—Ernest Hemingway, Jack Kerouac, Kurt Cobain, and Amy Winehouse, for example—Dylan fared reasonably well. A big part of his relative success required deflecting the identities and projections that were hurled in his direction. But many of these projections became so entwined with his image that they were impossible to shake, turning him into a palimpsest of claims and counterclaims that distorted and fragmented the living and breathing man into a web of contested meanings.

Consequently, from an outsider's perspective, it's hard to know where Dylan ends and the rumor mill of celebrity culture begins. There have been rumors of all types: secret marriages and births, sleazy womanizing, palimony suits, unflattering memoirs (the majority of which Dylan's lawyers have successfully barred from publication), tabloid tell-all's, creative nadirs and zeniths, drunken concert appearances, drug addiction, and frighteningly obsessive fans who have tried to forcibly remove his mask. Take, for example, Alan Jules Weberman. Described by Robert Shelton as "a would-be anarchist star, a wheeler-dealer of the freaked-out New Left," Weberman spent several years in the late Sixties and early Seventies harassing Dylan by repeatedly digging through his garbage, phoning him at all hours of the day and night, and leading agitated mobs to his Greenwich Village home to demand that he stop shirking his duties as the conscience of a generation. Such incursions have become a fact of life. Dylan's personal attorney, David Braun, is quoted by Clinton Heylin as saying, "In my twenty-two years' experience of representing famous personages no other person-ality has attracted such attention, nor created such a demand for information about his personal affairs."

Dylan's identity as a shape-changing performance artist also makes him hard to pin down. Long captivated by the figure of the American minstrel, his musical identities have channeled the identities of a dustbowl Oakie, a Beat poet, a Nashville cat, a Civil War general, a Born Again evangelist, a delta bluesman, and—rather curiously—previous versions of himself. Albums like *Love and Theft* (2001) do as Dylan has always done: lifting liber-ally from traditional American music. Lyrics and melodies from the 1950s, 1940s, 1930s, and much earlier, flow through his songs like a Biblical deluge. Arguably Dylan's greatest artistic contribu-tion has been his ability to appropriate and synthesize American traditions—folk, bluegrass, rock, gospel, etc.—and assume the real and imagined personae that accompany them.

As I suggested at the onset of this chapter, these musical and lyrical quotations aren't only a form of postmodern blackface. Although there's little doubt that some of his masks are the cal-culated stunts and tricks of a wily performance artist, his appro-priations are important expressions of his deeper sense of self and identity. Identity (whether artistic or personal), after all, isn't a dis-crete entity that seamlessly develops as we travel through life but is instead an amalgamation of perceptions, feelings, memories, symbols, and narratives in a dynamic state of flux and reinvention. In the words of Sam Shepard, who chronicled Dylan's Rolling Thunder Revue in 1975: "Dylan has ... made himself up from scratch. That is, from the things he had around him and inside him. Dylan is an invention of his own mind."

But those who are critical of his appropriations remain unconvinced. Even the satirical American newspaper, *The Onion*, took a swipe at the aging rock star when it ran an article in 2013 entitled "Bob Dylan Lays Off 2,000 Workers from Songwriting Factory." And shortly after the publication of *Chronicles: Volume One* in 2004, various blogs began reporting that passages from the book were lifted outright, or at least heavily influenced, by an array of unacknowledged literary sources that included Mark Twain, Jack London, F. Scott Fitzgerald, and Marcel Proust. For instance, Dylan describes writing the song "Political World" from the 1989 album *Oh Mercy* after a protracted creative dry spell:

> One night when everyone was asleep and I was sitting at the kitchen table, nothing on the hillside but a shiny bed of lights...

Compare this wording to language from Chapter 12 of *The Adventures of Huckleberry Finn*:

> Every night we passed towns, some of them away up on black hillsides, nothing but just a shiny bed of lights, not a house could you see.... There warn't a sound there; everybody was asleep...

Or read Nick Caraway's description of the drums of Gatsby's destiny against Dylan's account of leaving Minnesota for New York. Both men come from northern Minnesota; both change their names and assume self-fashioned identities as the result of an overwhelming sense of personal destiny. Fitzgerald has

Gatsby leave St. Olaf College in southern Minnesota, writing: "An instinct toward his future glory had led him, some months before, to the small Lutheran college of St. Olaf in southern Minnesota. He stayed there two weeks, dismayed at its ferocious indifference to the drums of his destiny, to destiny itself" (Fitzgerald, 1925, 99). Likewise, Dylan left the University of Minnesota after a few semesters to fulfill his own personal destiny out east.

Similar allegations were made about the albums *Love and Theft,* which borrowed liberally from Junichi Saga's *Confessions of a Yakuza*, and *Modern Times*, which lifted a slew of lines from the nineteenth-century confederate poet Henry Timrod, among other sources. The extent of these appropriations has become even more evident in the digital age, when a simple click of a button can reveal hundreds of textual matches. In a remarkable put-down in 2010, fellow songwriter and Rolling Thunder troubadour Joni Mitchell told the *Los Angeles Times* that Dylan was disingenuous through and through. "He's a plagiarist," she claimed, "and his name and voice are fake. Everything about Bob *is* deception."

Dylan responded to such allegations angrily while talking to Mikal Gilmore in 2012, saying, "Wussies and pussies complain about that stuff. It's an old thing—it's part of the tradition. It goes way back. These are the same people who tried to pin the name of Judas on me.[5] Judas, the most hated name in human history!

---

5. Dylan was called "Judas" by an angry member of the audience at a gig in Manchester in 1966. Caught on both tape and film, this moment is often cited as a more extreme example of the flack Dylan received for pushing the boundaries of folk music by splitting his live shows into acoustic and electric sets.

If you think you've been called a bad name, try to work your way out from under that. Yeah, and for what? For playing an electric guitar? As if that is in some kind of way equitable to betraying our Lord and delivering him up to be crucified. All those evil mother-fuckers can rot in hell."

Despite the tomes dedicated to his private affairs, Dylan is adamant that no man knows his history. As early as 1964, he announced to a sold-out Carnegie Hall on Halloween night that "I have my Bob Dylan mask on." Psychobiography thankfully doesn't get hung up on the historical accuracy of a life story. Masks are revealing. A psychobiographer is more interested in the themes and structures of a life narrative that shed light on the mind and life-world behind the story. Appropriating, embellishing, misrepresenting, fantasizing, projecting, and contradicting are all par for the course within the narrative realm. We all engage in these practices to varying degrees. Freud wrote that lying was a form of truth-telling because "false" memories frequently reveal more about a person than so-called "true" memories. The American writer Truman Capote, for example, often shared a memory of being at a zoo with his nanny on a day when two lions escaped their cages, prompting his nanny to run away, leaving him to wander around the zoo alone and vulnerable. Although this event most likely never took place, it communicates a great deal about who Capote was and how he felt about the world. The *psychological truth* that a given story conveys is considerably more valuable from a study of lives perspective than its *historical truth*. And so it's to *psychological truth* that we now turn.

Method

Over the course of this book, I draw on an interpretive phenomenological approach (IPA)[6] to examine how Bob Dylan *himself*
(as opposed to his interpreters and hagiographers) has made sense
of three major turning points: the aftermath of his 1966 motorcycle "accident," his Born Again conversion experience in 1978,
and his recommitment to songwriting and performing in 1987.

In his only complete case study, *Letters from Jenny* (1965),
Harvard personality psychologist Gordon Allport characterized
what he referred to as "the existentialist-oriented researcher" as
one who tried to compose, order, and extract the essence of a
subject's worldview in a manner that "would always place central
reliance on [the subject's] story, and would seek the explanation
for her [his] life in this summary worldview" (Allport, 1965,
164). Allport didn't believe that this explanation precluded
looking "into, around, through, and between" evidence to wager
an interpretation of the life. Such a wager involves alternating
between what the narrative psychologist Ruthellen Josselson
(2004) calls a hermeneutics of faith and a hermeneutics of suspicion. A hermeneutics of faith reconstructs what a subject says
about his or her life and its sources of meaning. The act is largely
one of representation. A hermeneutics of suspicion, on the other
hand, looks beneath the surface for depth realities of which the

6. Larkin, M., Watts, S., Clifton, E. (2006). "Giving Voice and Making Sense in
Interpretative Phenomenological Analysis." *Qualitative Research in Psychology, 3*(2),
102–120.

subject may not be conscious: gaps, silences, and attempts at obfuscation.

Phenomenological psychology traces its roots back to the philosophical writings of Edmund Husserl (1859–1938) and his student Martin Heidegger (1889–1976). Similar to Allport's "existentialist" approach, its principal goal is to capture a person's experiences of self, others, and world as faithfully as possible. Rather than an overreliance on psychological theory and experimental data, priority is given to a person's own idiosyncratic perspectives and interpretations. Phenomenologists aim to reveal subject matter—for example, the experience of receiving an HIV-positive diagnosis, heroin addiction, lymphoma, love, etc.—on its own terms, not according to a preconceived set of assumptions.

In my teaching practice, I've used the American writer Raymond Carver's short story "What We Talk About When We Talk About Love" to illuminate the merits of phenomenological analyses. In this modern day *Symposium*, four friends sit around a kitchen table with a bottle of gin discussing their understandings of love. One of the friends, Terri, had an abusive relationship and continues to associate her ex-boyfriend's violent outbursts with love. Mel, who is currently married to Terri, explains how his work as an emergency room surgeon informs his understanding by telling a story about an elderly couple that survived injuries from a serious automobile accident because of having each other to live for. An acrimonious divorce earlier in life also taught him that people grieve lost love but eventually move on. By the end of the story, the friends find themselves unsettled by the differences between their conceptions of an emotional and mental state that's anything but univocal. Knowledge of what they actually mean when they talk about love reveals a good deal about the people they are and why they think what they think about the world.

Once the descriptive work of phenomenology is done, the challenging interpretive work begins. When trying to interpret the narrative and behavioral traces of a life, psychobiographers sleuth around for what the psychologist Irving Alexander called *psychological saliencies*. Doing the same things over and over, repeating stories, or acting in predictable ways may signal core conflicts, concerns, or themes that warrant further investigation. Dylan, as I mentioned at the beginning of the chapter, has frequently appealed to *destiny* when explaining why he has remained in a state of becoming. "I was heading for the fantastic lights. No doubt about it," he writes in *Chronicles* of his early days in New York City. "Could it be that I was being deceived? Not likely. I don't think I had enough imagination to be deceived; had no false hope, either. I'd come from a long ways off and had started from a long ways down. But now destiny was about to manifest itself. I felt like it was looking right at me and nobody else" (Dylan, 2004, 22).

Destiny is defined in theology as a predetermined course of events and is often used synonymously with fate or fortune. It's often conceived of as a divine plan or inner voice guiding people through the randomness of worldly affairs. In the *Summa Theologica*, Thomas Aquinas, for instance, argued that the destiny of a creature was either proportionate to its created nature or could exceed that nature. It could exceed nature if the creature experienced a vision of God and eternal life that moved it to grow beyond the state it had been born into. But as William James pointed out in *The Varieties of Religious Experience* (1902), defining religious phenomenology categorically was problematic because all religious experiences are blended with the psychosocial realities of the persons living through them. Developmental, cultural, psychodynamic, and dispositional variables invariably shape religious experience. A Christian's image of Christ will vary based on a host of personal and sociocultural variables. The same can be said of Jewish understandings of what it means to be a chosen people or Muslim perspectives on the meanings of Jihad.

Dylan has explained his changes using a whole web of related words over the years: as destiny, primarily, but also as a line, a gift, a calling, self-fulfillment, as self-knowledge, as having been chosen for something by a higher power, as doing God's work, as inevitability, and as a source of direction. All of these words intimate a belief in a supreme power—or, in the words of Dylan, "a God of time and space"—that creates people with specific destinies in mind. Given the transience of time and precariousness of life, people must actualize *who they are* before it's too late. As a basis for personal identity, this notion is Biblical. Whether in the Talmud or the Pauline Epistles, the search for "*who I am*" is expressed as a search for "*what I am*," vocationally speaking.

In a May 1963 interview on Chicago's WFMT with the legendary Studs Terkel, Dylan was asked about what led him to songwriting. *Freewheelin'* was about to be released and Albert Grossman had scheduled an out-of-town appearance at a new folk club in the Windy City—The Bear—in addition to an appearance on Terkel's *Wax Museum* radio show.[7] During the interview, Dylan characterized himself as "one of these people that think

7. A recorder of oral histories and adept social commentator, Terkel commanded a large listening audience across the Midwest.

everybody has certain gifts, you know, when they're born, and you got enough trouble just trying to find out what it is. I used to play the guitar when I was ten, you know. So I figured maybe that's my little gift. Like somebody can make a cake, or somebody else can saw a tree down, and other people write. . . . I had seen that this is exactly what my gift is, maybe I got a better gift. But as of right now, I haven't found out what it is. I don't call it a gift, it's only my way of trying to explain something that is very hard to explain."

The importance of discovering *what he is* comes up obsessively during his early interviews. In November 1964, for instance, he told the *Kenyon Collegian*: "You can't learn to be someone else. It's just got to be inside." And two years later, he'd tell Robert Shelton: "You just have to make it. When I say 'make it', I don't mean being a popular folk-rock star. Making it means finding your line. Everybody's line is there, someplace."

Considering its saliency within his narrative of self, Dylan's experiences and representations of "destiny" warrant investigation. Do specific cognitive/affective structures and processes undergird it? Is it relatively static or has it signified different things to him at different times? During an appearance on *60 Minutes* in December 2004, the late Ed Bradley asked Dylan what he meant by it. Evoked in the passage from *Chronicles* quoted earlier, Dylan is asked to clarify. Dressed nattily in a black velour suit with a neat haircut, his sharp blue eyes looking unflinchingly ahead, he answers with aphoristic restraint, describing destiny as "a feeling you have that you know something about yourself that nobody else does. The picture you have in your mind of what you're about *will* come true." Across the chapters that follow, I hope to show that although this picture of self has changed considerably for Dylan

over the years, each of his major changes possesses a similar underlying structure—or a *script*.

Theory

Getting a feel for the structure of someone's life narrative helps
make his or her contradictions, ambiguities, and silences read
more coherently. According to script theory (conceived of by
Silvan Tomkins), personality is best thought of as an open set of
stimulus-affect-response sequences that repeat across time and
reveal the "deep structure" of a life. The basic unit of analysis for
scripting is a *scene*. A scene is best understood as a "happening"
that includes persons, time, actions, and affect. A *script*, on the
other hand, consists of an individual's rules for the prediction, interpretation, and control of experiences governed by a "family" of
related scenes held together by a narrative.

We all have scripts that play out in our lives. Real or imagined
things happen and produce sets of emotions, thoughts, and behaviors that are often repetitious and therefore predictable. For
example, in his psychobiography of John Lennon (2013), Tim
Kasser locates a script in Lennon's famous song "Lucy in the Sky
with Diamonds" that he also finds in earlier songs, in addition
to tracing it through Lennon's life story. The script reflects a
man who was preoccupied with a connection to and separation
from an incredible female endowed with life-restoring powers.
Kasser connects this script to Lennon's feelings about his mother,
Julia, who died after being struck by a car when he was eighteen
years old.

"Scripting" by Tomkins involves locating the pattern underlying the repetitious story. If the script does in fact reveal a person's "identity story," it can be found in an array of contexts—within the realm of self-descriptions, in the stories that we tell about other people, and in those external narratives that we express interest in. And if we happen to be novelists, poets, lyrical songwriters, or dramatists, scripts often weasel their way into the texts that we write.

The script I discovered amidst Dylan's self-explanations comes in variations of the following structure:

> *I have lost my sense of identity and purpose. I feel anxious and*
> *vulnerable to death and destruction. I turn to the songs and*
> *artists of my youth for guidance. I feel a redeemed sense of self*
> *and purpose. I reflect upon the change and understand it as the*
> *process of developing into who I'm supposed to be. . . .*

Put more organically, Bob Dylan has returned to the musical figures and traditions of his youth, heard on vinyl records and over the AM radio, at points in his life when death and destruction (whether real or imagined) threaten his sense of purpose of safety. These musical traditions and their colorful personae have consistently provided an evolving self-picture that safeguards him from anxiety. A full or partial version of this script, which I'll hereafter refer to as *the destiny script*, is often embedded in Dylan's self-explanations of change. He calls it destiny, but that's a metonym for something else, something deeper, something he purports not to fully understand himself.

Tomkins believed that key scenes from our early childhoods were often *magnified* by strong positive emotions (principally joy or excitement) or strong negative emotions (such as fear, sadness, anger, guilt, shame, or disgust) and then reinforced by stimuli within our environments. A scene magnified by overwhelmingly negative emotion has a good chance of becoming salient. Once that happened, a cognitive/affective schema could crystalize around it in the form of a family of scenes—possibly developing into what Tomkins called a *nuclear script*. The primary characteristic of a nuclear script was an unrecoverable longing for a lost paradise, something good having turned bad. But the hope for the good life can't be relinquished, so the nuclearized scene becomes endlessly haunting. A script will persist over time provided that analogs are formed between the original family of scenes and subsequent experiences. In other words, new experiences are unconsciously surveyed for old disappointments and dangers. If such forces are detected, the psyche will process the new experience according to the schema of the script.

Tomkins identified a class of scripts that he named *reparative scripts* in which a person attempts to move beyond or recontextualize a threatening scene. In such scripts, the analogs of threatening scenes were resolved by anti-analogs, which are idealized scenes that assuage destruction and danger through a redemptive vision of the good life. Something of negative value is turned into something of positive value and the self benefits in the end, even if only temporarily. The narrative psychologist Dan McAdams (2006) has since renamed this script a *redemptive script*. McAdams argues that the personal stories of individuals who score high on markers of generativity frequently revolve around redemptive sequences in which pain, suffering, and death are confronted and overcome. This type of narrative, argues McAdams, is "as American as Apple pie, the Super Bowl, and manifest destiny." It can be found in John Winthrop's *City Upon a Hill* (1630) and in the life story of Oprah Winfrey. Whether in an economic form (e.g., a rags to riches story), an emancipatory one (e.g., nineteenth-century slave narratives), or a psychiatric one (e.g., Prozac literature), the redemptive self moves from adversity to salvation.

Likewise, many of Bob Dylan's personal stories of transformation are redemptive in form and theme. A combination of feeling lost and a deeply internalized fear of death/apocalypse prompts a crisis of identity and purpose that presses for resolution. His vivid childhood memories of Cold War air raid drills and underlying threat of nuclear annihilation are mitigated by the "sonic" salvation that crackled through his radio speakers late at night from Shreveport, Louisiana. Of his childhood and its anxieties, Dylan writes in *Chronicles*: "Back then when something was wrong the radio could lay hands on you and you'd be all right" (Dylan, 2004, 188). His most steadfast sense of identity was guided by the imaginative worlds that came to life through the blues, gospel, Appalachian, and country music that he heard and ended up playing himself. When asked by Ed Bradley about what impelled him to follow his musical dreams, Dylan responded, "I listened to the radio a lot. I hung out in the record stores. And I slam-banged around on the guitar and played the piano and learned songs from a world which didn't exist around me." His evolving identity was driven more by his investment in this ghostly sound than by any rationalized set of aesthetic or political principles. At the center of this investment was the impulse to connect with cultural traditions that predated his birth, which is likely the same general impulse behind his lifelong interests in Judaism and Christianity.

Interestingly, an extended form of the destiny script is strewn throughout a book that Dylan was endorsing to friends and acquaintances in the early Nineties, around the time he was studying with Rabbis associated with the Chabad Lubavitch movement of Hasidic Judaism. According to Dylan's New York associate and acquaintance Raymond Foye, there was something about Isaac Bashevis Singer's 1962 novel *The Slave* that stopped Dylan in his tracks, something hauntingly familiar.

The story centers on a Polish Jew named Jacob who is displaced from his hometown of Josefov after the Khmelnytsky massacres of the seventeenth century, during which an estimated one thousand Jewish men, women, and children were slaughtered by Cossacks. Exiled from his homeland and sold into slavery, Jacob attempts to reclaim the rituals and stories of Jewish tradition through memory, even trying to etch the Torah into a rock. He eventually falls in love with a gentile named Wanda, the daughter of his master, and helps convert her to Judaism. Caught between the Jewish and Gentile worlds, Jacob and Wanda must reinvent themselves as a means of fulfilling their destiny to live freely as husband and wife. Literary critics have characterized the novel as an allegorical meditation on the Nazi Holocaust and the struggle of Jewish identity and transmission within the mid-twentieth century diaspora.

The narrative of exile and return, which is so central to Judaism, has always played a role within Bob Dylan's life story and art. It's a narrative that reverberates through an abundance of traditional American music, especially the blues and Gospel that he grew up listening to over the radio. Interesting lines of continuity exist between the themes of death and renewal within the Talmudic Judaism practiced by Dylan's ancestors and the spiritual songs of conflict and redemption that emerged out of American slavery. It shouldn't be surprising then that Dylan would claim after his Jesus experience in 1978 that he was both Jewish and Christian and that there was no fundamental contradiction between what he read in the Jewish Bible and what he discovered later in the New Testament. The spiritual dimensions of the destiny script and its bases within Judeo-Christian traditions are essential to understanding Dylan's personal and artistic changes—changes that took on a distinctively Christian character during the late-1970s.

The French novelist Marcel Proust believed that, for an artist, the moments of a life remained unfinished until they had the occasion to be transposed into art. Works of art play significant roles in creating their creators. Along these lines, Bob Dylan's shifting self-expressions are inexorably linked to his creative work. In particular, it has been the poetry of his lyrics that has helped to propel his metamorphoses into being. As he put it in response to the 1963 *Newsweek* article, "I am my words." The lyrics to many of his songs contain themes of death, rebirth, and metamorphosis, especially the ones he composed during or immediately after periods of acute transition and change.

Irving Alexander believed that saliencies could be found in many places, including habitual trips to the same vacation spot, the reading and rereading of the same book over a period of years, and repetitive behaviors—all were potential sources of information about the dynamics of someone's inner life. Artists offer psychologists a great deal in way of saliencies. Recurring motifs, storylines, and images often indicate an underlying preoccupation.

Given the voluminous and multifaceted nature of Dylan's discography, locating saliencies can lead to oversimplification. In any case, there are reliable ways of searching for them. The frequency with which Dylan has performed a given song and/or the enthusiasm with which he has spoken or written about it may offer revealing information about his well-guarded inner life. Over the following three chapters, I will highlight a trio of songs that are salient—"I Shall Be Released" (1967), "In the Garden" (1979), and "Where Teardrops Fall" (1989)—each of which was written and recorded after one of the three turning points taken up in this book and each of which Dylan himself seems to have had a special affinity for. What's more, the three songs build on one another to tell a Bible-infused story that mirrors Dylan's own jagged experience of struggle, destiny, and transformation.

The themes of death and rebirth in these songs were no doubt inspired by multiple sources, including developmental changes, periods of sobriety, and events in his romantic/personal life. Time and time again, however, his more redemptive compositions feature a return to musical roots. On many occasions, Dylan has referred to "those old songs," which is his name for an idiosyncratic canon of music to which he has always been faithful. According to him, whenever he has strayed from the melodies and principles of "those old songs," his music and life have gone off course. Their lyrics, melodies, arrangements, and histories have consistently influenced Dylan's sense of self and direction. "I learned lyrics and how to write them from listening to folk songs," Dylan said in 2015. "And I played them, and

I met other people that played them back when nobody was doing it. Sang nothing but these folk songs, and they gave me the code for everything that's fair game, that everything belongs to everyone."

When asked about his religious views by the *New York Times* in 1997, Dylan responded psychologically: "You can find all my philosophy in those old songs. I believe in a God of time and space, but if people ask me about that, my impulse is to point them back toward those songs. I believe in Hank Williams singing 'I Saw the Light'. I've seen the light, too." The old songs offered him visions from a world that no longer existed, a spiritual way forward in a world plagued by "power and greed and corruptible seed." What's important here is that Hank Williams's song didn't simply influence Dylan's guitar playing or vocal technique, but it suggested an orientation in the world that felt more authentic than the one he was living. The signs, symbols, sounds, lyrics, and Biblical roots of "those old songs" have mediated his evolving self-understandings, leading him onward in his journey, offering him refuge from stagnation, fear, and death. It's to the dial of the radio and its salvific powers that he has turned during times of worry. Take the rough-and-tumble middle verse of the bluesy 2001 song "Lonesome Day Blues," written shortly after the death of his beloved mother, Beatty, in 2000:

I'm forty miles from the mill—I'm droppin' it into overdrive
I'm forty miles from the mill—I'm droppin' it into overdrive
Settin' my dial on the radio
I wish my mother was still alive

And the radio for Dylan is always only a half-step from his guitar, piano, and a notebook of lyrical jottings and jags penned in his microscopic script.

Useful in this context is the postmodern French philosopher Paul Ricoeur (1970), who developed a double hermeneutics of regression and progression to help conceptualize how artists use creative projects to transpose core-level preoccupations into new life-affirming forms. Improving on Freud's monograph on Leonardo Da Vinci (1910), Ricoeur demonstrated how regressive psychological energies, which in Leonardo's case may have been an unresolved Oedipal complex, were transformed through the progressive solution of his activities as an artist and scientist. Ricoeur asks, "Could it be that the true meaning of sublimation is to promote new meanings by mobilizing old energies initially invested in archaic figures?" (Ricoeur, 1970, 175). This mobilization was thought by Ricoeur to take place whenever a person used words, images, music, or stories to advance his or her consciousness to a new understanding of the self and world.

The dynamics behind this "advancement" are psychologically revealing because they expose the tension between *archeology* (the regressive and unresolvable conflicts of one's childhood) and *teleology* (the progressive impulse to move beyond "archaic figures"). Ricoeur shows how works of art such as Michelangelo's *Moses*, Sophocles' *Oedipus Rex*, and Shakespeare's *Hamlet*, reveal dialectics between the innermost conflicts of the artists and those solutions enacted by the creative process. The dialectical tension between archeology and teleology led to the creation of something that wasn't there before, an artifact, or what Jean-Paul Sartre

(1968) called *the progressive project*.[8] In Dylan's case, the transfigured self that emerges out of a significant change becomes realized through the music he composes, records, and performs immediately after the change. As he explained to journalists after his Born Again experience in 1978, if people really wanted to know what he felt, they should listen to his songs.

If scripting reveals the "deep structure" of a life, and if Ricoeur's double hermeneutics helps draw attention to the lived permutations of this structure, important questions remain about the sociocultural realities that shape the person. Robert J. Lifton's concepts of atomic anxiety and the protean self shed valuable historical light on the origins of the destiny script. According to Lifton (1979), many Americans whose lives coincided with the middle part of the twentieth century were besieged by feelings of rootlessness and affected by images of widespread extinction through mass media. A capacity to be multifaceted and changeable, or *protean*, had become increasingly necessary for psychosocial survival. In addition to putting together disparate elements of identity into "odd combinations" and frequently changing these elements, the protean self took on the psychology of a survivor and underwent symbolic forms of death and rebirth.

The portrait that will emerge from this book is of a private, eccentric, and work-obsessed celebrity musician whose artistic changes have been impelled by a deeply personal relationship to American musical traditions during an age of apocalyptic threat

8. Sartre writes: "For us man is characterized above all by his going beyond a situation, and by what he succeeds in making of what he has been made—even if he never recognizes himself in his objectification" (Sartre, 1968, 109).

and dislocation. Dylan's early life growing up in the atrophying iron range of Minnesota during the Cold War, the grandson of Jewish émigrés who fled Russia after anti-Semitic pogroms, helps shed some light on his remarkable level of changeability as an artist.

Layout of the Book

Chapters 2–4 explore the presence of the destiny script through the three turning points mentioned earlier: the aftermath of Dylan's 1966 motorcycle "accident," his Born Again conversion experience in 1978, and his recommitment to songwriting and performing in 1987. Each of these chapters provides some biographical context, followed by a close reading of interviews and autobiographical writings in which the script is present. I then draw on decades of critical writing on Dylan's work to offer general analyses of some of the creative work that followed the change. As mentioned earlier, each of the following three chapters will include a close examination of a song that Dylan has signaled was especially meaningful for him to write and perform. Chapter 5 uses the work of Robert J. Lifton on the psychological effects of Cold War-era apocalyptic anxiety to help contextualize the death threat that runs through Dylan's life and music and that factors prominently in his transformational tendencies. A larger cultural explanation will help grant the topsy-turvy swerve of Dylan's works and days a historical shape. The final chapter draws on some identity theory to conceptualize how Dylan's relationship to "tradition" (as he defines it) has factored into his continually changing expression of self.

2 | THE MOTORCYCLE CRACK UP

The dream of man's heart, however much he may distrust and resent it, is that life may complete itself in significant pattern. Some incomprehensible way. Before death.

—Saul Bellow

Within a few years of being signed to Columbia Records, fame knocked Dylan off his feet and dragged him into an exciting new life. The kid who had written in his senior yearbook in 1959 that his ambition was "To join Little Richard" had accomplished that in a mere four years time.[1] Flashbulbs were popping and journalists wanted to know his thoughts on music, politics, and life. In addition to his prolific and deeply affecting songwriting, Dylan's charisma and iconoclastic behavior attracted significant media attention. For example, on May 12, 1963, he walked out of an Ed Sullivan Show taping when the head of program practices tried to keep him from playing the potentially libelous "Talkin' John Birch Society Blues." The following December, three weeks after President Kennedy was killed

1. He reported to a friend that by 1963 his fame had grown so much that he had to begin walking around concerts and festivals wearing a disguise.

in Dallas, he shocked the well-to-do left-wing Emergency Civil Liberties Committee, which was presenting him its annual Tom Paine award, by drunkenly declaring that he no longer saw things in terms of black and white, or left and right, claiming that— "there's only up and down." He then proceeded to upset the audience further by deriding them as old and out of touch and saying that, as a young man, he saw something of himself in Lee Harvey Oswald.

As the orbit of his influence expanded beyond the streets of Greenwich Village, former champions of his in the folk world began expressing disapproval. In response to the nontopical songs featured on *Another Side of Bob Dylan*, released in August 1964, Irwin Silber, editor of the famed folk magazine *Sing Out!*, published an open letter criticizing Dylan for eschewing protest songs in favor of selfish introspection. He was disappointed by Dylan's aloof presence at that summer's Newport Folk Festival. "I saw at Newport how you had somehow lost contact with people," wrote Silber, adding disparagingly that Bob was now traveling with an entourage of drinking buddies, referring to Dylan's sharp-tongued New York City posse that included the acerbic Bobby Neuwirth and the hulking Victor Maymudes. By many accounts, he'd shed his boyish charm and had become moody, withdrawn, and dismissive of those who either stood in his way or who wanted something from him.

From the release of *Another Side* until his accident two years later, Dylan's life spiraled out of control. His Icarus-like rise and fall was in many ways fomented by the writing of "Like a Rolling Stone," an event he characterized in interviews as an artistic breakthrough—describing a frenzied writing session of the likes of Jack Kerouac that led to page after page of lyrics and scribbles: "…it was ten pages long, it wasn't called anything, just a rhythm thing on paper, all about my steady hatred, directed at some point that was honest," Dylan explained in 1966.

"Like a Rolling Stone," the first track on *Highway 61 Revisited*, was recorded on June 16, 1965, and released as a single on July 20, a month in advance of the groundbreaking album. Four days after its release, the song roared onto the American charts. And a few days after that, Dylan caused a stir by playing his famous three-song set of amplified rock-n-roll at his third Newport Folk Festival.

The performance was a confusing event that delighted some and disappointed others, especially the event organizers and folk patriarchs. One persistent legend has it that an irate Pete Seeger threatened to cut the sound cables with an axe because the lyrics couldn't be deciphered amidst the crackling distortion. Regardless of whether Dylan was booed or not, and to what degree, his status as a celebrity rock star was unquestionable. He suddenly had more in common (at least professionally) with The Beatles and The Rolling Stones than with Peter, Paul, and Mary, Alan Lomax, or Seeger. Publishing executives offered him large advances to write a book. A steady stream of adoring women wanted to sleep with him. Promoters tried to woo him into their venues. And although he was jeered at times for "selling out," fans continued to show up at his concerts and hangers-on accumulated around him like moths around a flame.

On the heels of Newport, Dylan took his new electric band (the Hawks from outside Toronto) on the road for a world tour comprised of forty-seven dates crisscrossing the United States,

Canada, Australia, Sweden, Denmark, Ireland, England, Wales, Scotland, and France. During a hiatus in November 1965, he secretly married Sara Lownds, who was pregnant with their first child, then hit the road again, telling virtually no one of his marriage. Dylan and Sara had met sometime in 1962 in New York City when she was still married to her first husband, a much older fashion photographer named Hans Lownds, whom she ended up leaving for Dylan. A beautiful woman with pale skin, dark hair, and striking eyes, she'd worked at the New York Playboy Club as a bunny girl before becoming a fashion model represented by the Ford Agency. Dylan and Sara became romantic sometime in 1964 and were married the following year in a quiet ceremony on Long Island. A few months later, in May 1966, the road-weary and strung out twenty-five-year-old Dylan returned from Europe and was looking down the barrel of a grueling American leg of sixty-four shows scheduled to kick off in New Haven, Connecticut. These dates weren't his only pressing obligation at the time. He'd accepted a generous $10,000 advance from the Macmillan Company for the novel that would eventually be published as *Tarantula* in 1970, a Beat-inspired surrealist collection of disjointed vignettes that Dylan has always had ambivalent feelings about. He'd written a draft that the editors seemed happy enough with, but something about the manuscript irked him, and so he dragged a typewriter along on tour with the hopes of producing something worthy of publication. Nothing agreeable came of his efforts and Macmillan was chomping at the bit for their manuscript. Furthermore, ABC was waiting for a documentary called *Eat the Document* that D. A. Pennebaker had shot in addition to the footage that made it into *Dont Look Back*.

Responsibilities, amphetamines, fame, and near-constant touring were propelling the young rock star in a dangerous direction. Fellow Greenwich Village folk musician Phil Ochs foresaw the crisis that was consuming his friend. "I wonder what's going to happen," Ochs said in print. "I don't know if Dylan can get on the stage a year from now. I don't think so. I mean the phenomenon of Dylan will be so much that it will be dangerous. . . . Dylan has become part of so many people's psyches—and there're so many screwed up people in America, and death is such a part of the American scene now." Ochs' concern was prescient.

News then came over the radios of America on Friday July 29, 1966, that Bob Dylan had been seriously injured in a motorcycle accident in Woodstock, New York, where he'd been living on and off since 1964. The celebrity rumor mill began churning out stories that he was disfigured, paralyzed from the neck down, comatose, or possibly dead. His own parents, Abe and Beatty, heard the news over the radio and placed several panicked calls from out west to inquire about their son. To this day, no one other than Dylan and Sara has a clear sense of the specifics. According to biographer Daniel Epstein (and others), Dylan was walking his cumbersome Triumph 500 motorcycle from his manager Albert Grossman's garage in Bearsville down Striebel Road toward Glasco Turnpike. The tires on the motorcycle were flat and he was wheeling it out to be repaired. Sara was following him in a car. At some point, he apparently lost his balance on the wet road and the heavy motorcycle fell down on top of him. It was hardly an accident reminiscent of the fiery deaths of James Dean or Dylan's friend Richard Fariña, author of the cult classic *Been Down So Long It Looks Like Up to Me* and husband of Mimi Baez, sister of Joan Baez. No police were summoned to Bearsville, and there's no record of Dylan being taken to the local hospital in Kingston, New York, despite his later claiming that he was hospitalized for a week.

Instead, Sara seems to have driven her husband fifty miles south to Middletown to the large Victorian home of Dr. Edward Thayer, who, incidentally, had a reputation for helping people detox from drugs. Thayer and his wife, Selma, made up a room for their celebrity guest on the third floor. He recovered there for an extended period of time, frequently visited by Sara and some-times his kids, and then moved back to Woodstock for more rest. Gradually, he allowed a small number of friends and associates to visit him. Journalist and friend Al Aronowitz came to see him shortly after the accident and thought it was a put on. According to him, Dylan was in "pretty good shape." D. A. Pennebaker had a similar report after his visit: "He didn't appear very knocked out by the accident," he told Clinton Heylin.

Regardless of whether the accident is best understood in terms of physical or psychic injuries (or a combination), and whether these injuries were sustained on the morning of Friday July 29, 1966 or over the months and years leading up to that fateful morning, Dylan underwent a change that many fans, followers, and friends noticed. And it's a change that he has always been hesi-tant to talk about at length.

The Script

At the heart of the *destiny script* is a key scene in which Dylan's life is thrown into real or imagined jeopardy. This, as I will explain in Chapter 5, can be traced back to a cluster of experiences growing up culturally Jewish during the early years of the Cold War. According to Tomkins (1995), once again, a scene permeated by negative affect becomes magnified when it forms *analogs* in which new situations are imbued with the fears and dangers of the original scene. If magnified significantly, the scene may join into a family of interconnected scenes called a script, which orders future life events according to its own set of internal rules. In Dylan's case, this family of related scenes usually includes a "liminal" scene in which he finds himself between things (e.g., between legs of a tour, between recording projects, between relationships, or between life phases), a scene of threat or imminent danger, and a "self-discovery" scene—in which he temporarily resolves his fear of annihilation by assuming an identity and sense of purpose born out of the country, blues, and folk sounds and stories that exhilarated him as a kid in Minnesota.

A key belief in script theory is that the development of personality doesn't involve a point-for-point progression from earlier to later constructions of a nuclear scene and its accompanying script. Although scenes and scripts usually retain a core structure, constructions of the past are revised, diminished, and augmented by subsequent life experiences. This "partially open and partially closed system" allows one to anticipate, respond to, and control events meaningfully. Across the pages that follow, I present three partial descriptions of the motorcycle accident recounted by Dylan in 1969, 1987, and 2012. Although the three vary in the level of their completeness, they all contain versions of the destiny script as it has waxed and waned over time. Of particular interest is how the script takes on an increasingly religious form as time passes.

November 1969

Dylan discussed the accident for the first time publicly in a sprawling 1969 interview with Jann Wenner of *Rolling Stone*. After trying to schedule the interview for eighteen months, Wenner finally secured a meeting in New York City, on the same day that Judy Garland's body was being viewed by thousands of mourners and fans at a funeral home around the corner from the hotel where the interview took place. On several occasions, Wenner questions Dylan directly about the accident and the changes it led to. "What change? Well . . . it limited me," a cautious Dylan responds at one point. "It's hard to speak about the change, you know? It's not the type of change that one can put into words . . . besides the physical change. I had a busted vertebrae; neck vertebrae. And there's really not much to talk about. I don't want to talk about it."

But he does talk about it, albeit obliquely. He claims having felt adrift and worn down in the time leading up to the accident. Wenner asks early on why he stopped touring. Dylan replies, "well, Jann, I'll tell ya—I was on the road for almost five years. It wore me down. I was on drugs, a lot of things. A lot of things just to keep going, you know? And I don't want to live that way anymore. And uh . . . I'm just waiting for a better time—you know what I mean?"

As we'll repeatedly see across Dylan's life, a rudderless existence renders him vulnerable to the threat of death—which is precisely how the motorcycle accident enters into his narrative.

Dylan explains to Wenner that the crash occurred during a month-long vacation between legs of his tour, at the peak of his exhaustion. "At that time I had a dreadful motorcycle accident . . . which put me away for a while . . . and I still didn't sense the importance of that accident till at least a year after that. I realized that it was a *real* accident." Dylan follows this emphatic remark with a curious statement that suggests a loss of identity: "I mean I thought that I was just gonna get up and go back to doing what I was doing before . . . but I couldn't do it anymore."

Throughout the interview, he comes across as tentative and uncertain when answering questions about his pre-accident self. Whether it's erroneously claiming that John Hammond signed him to Columbia Records a year before he moved to New York City or forgetting which of his songs appear on which records, Dylan is shaky on dates and past motivations. When Wenner asks if he ever listens to his old albums, he even humorously refers to himself in the third person: "That's the way I listen to my records—every once in a while. Every once in a while I say 'Well, I'd like to see that fellow again.'"

Dylan remains vague when asked to explain his new musical style. But the previous year, in an interview with John Cohen and Happy Traum published in the October/November 1968 issue of *Sing Out!*, he is asked about music that reaches him. "Those old songs reach me," he answers. "I don't hear them as often as I used to. But like this other week, I heard on the radio Buell Kazee and he reached me." Buell Kazee (1900–76), a country and folk singer, was one of the most celebrated folk musicians of the 1920s, whom Dylan likely first encountered on Harry Smith's *Anthology of American Folk Music*. He goes on to list a whole slew of earlier

American and Anglo-Irish musical influences, including Scrapper Blackwell, Leroy Carr, Jack Dupree, Lonnie Johnson, Jelly Roll Morton, Buddy Bolden, Porter Wagoner, The Clancy Brothers, and Tommy Makem.

July 1987

Eighteen years later, the playwright and Rolling Thunder alumnus Sam Shepard published a one-act play in *Esquire* called *A Short Life of Trouble* based on a meandering interview he conducted with Dylan on topics ranging from James Dean to early musical influences, with particular attention paid to the tragic ends that many of these influences met. The theme of death pervades the conversation. Attention is paid to the tragic and/or painful deaths of Ricky Nelson, James Dean, Hank Williams, and Woody Guthrie. In the final exchanges, Shepard and Dylan take up his motorcycle accident. When asked by Shepard what happened, he responds enigmatically at first, saying, "I couldn't handle it. I was dumbstruck." "How do you mean?" inquires Shepard. "I just wasn't ready for it." Dylan then goes on to elaborate on how he was riding his Triumph 500 on top of a hill near Woodstock early one morning when "the big orange sun," which he looked up at directly, blinded him. ". . . I went blind for a second and I kind of panicked or something, I stomped down on the brake and the rear wheel locked up on me and I went flyin'."

He describes being knocked out cold and then spending a week in the hospital followed by a period of recovery in the attic of "this doctor's house in town." "I just started thinking about the short life of trouble," says Dylan, describing his psychological state while recovering in the doctor's attic. "How short life is. I'd just lay there listenin' to birds chirping. Kids playing in the neighbor's yard or rain falling by the window. I realized how much I'd missed. Then I'd hear the fire engine roar, and I could feel the steady thrust of death that had been constantly looking over its shoulder at me. . . ."

Although he doesn't discuss how he ultimately assuaged the threat of death, he talks earlier in the play about knowing his place vis-à-vis "the old forms" of traditional American music and how he'd hear certain songs over the radio growing up and imagine himself as the singer. "So, you'd mainly imagine the singer when you heard the song?" asks Shepard. "Yeah. A faceless singer," Dylan responds. "I'd fill in the face."

September 2012

In the 2012 *Rolling Stone* interview with Mikal Gilmore, Dylan referred to the accident and its aftermath as a "transfiguration." In the Gospels of Matthew, Mark, and Luke—all of which Dylan knows intimately after decades of Bible study—Jesus appears in radiant glory to three of his disciples and is forever changed in their eyes. Here's how it's described in the Gospel According to Matthew (17:2), Dylan's favorite gospel: "And he was transfigured before them [the disciples Peter, James, and John], and his face shone like the sun, and his clothes became dazzling white..."

"So when you ask some of your questions, you're asking them to a person who's long dead," Dylan explains to Gilmore. "You're asking them to a person who doesn't exist. . . . Transfiguration is what allows you to crawl out from under the chaos and fly above it." He goes on to cite the motorcycle accident as an example of the phenomenon. "...I had a motorcycle accident myself, in '66, so we're talking about two years—a gradual kind of slipping away, and, uh, some kind of something else appearing out of nowhere."

The phenomenon, as he has come to understand it, involves developing into the person that you're destined to become—and by doing so, actualizing the evolving picture you have in your mind of *who* you are and *what* you're about. In a 1985 interview with Bob Brown for ABC's *20/20*, he characterized earthly existence as "a place where you have to work certain things out." When asked what it was that he had to work out, Dylan responded, "Well, you have to work out where your place is, and who you are. But we're all spirit. That's all we are. We're just walking. We're just dressed up in a suit of skin. We're going to leave that behind."

In the *Rolling Stone* interview, Gilmore asks if he became "a different person" after the accident. Dylan's reply contains the ineffable quality present in many descriptions of quantum change. He says, "I'm trying to explain something that can't be explained. . . . Some people never really develop into who they're supposed to be. They get cut off. They go another way. It happens a lot. We all see people that that's happened to. We see them on the street. It's like they have a sign hanging on them." But Dylan suggests that he isn't like one of those people. He's one of the transfigured few.

The Progressive Project

After his initial recovery over the course of the summer of 1966, Dylan continued to write and record music but on his own terms. He was running over songs with The Hawks (soon to be renamed The Band), which had been retained by Columbia Records for the purposes of helping their prodigy churn out enough original material to meet his contractual obligation of one album per year. They set up a basement studio at a house they rented called Big Pink in nearby West Saugerties. It was an ideal setting for Dylan to regenerate artistically. "That's really the way to do a recording," he told Wenner in the 1969 interview detailed earlier, "in a peaceful, relaxed setting, in somebody's basement. With the windows open and a dog lying on the floor." Dylan fell into a flexible schedule where he'd get up early, make coffee, and sit at his typewriter composing lyrics. He'd then drive over to Big Pink to rehearse and record using two stereo mixers and a reel-to-reel tape recorder owned by Albert Grossman and a set of microphones loaned to them by Peter, Paul, and Mary.

Dylan, Robbie Robertson, Garth Hudson, Rick Danko, and Levon Helm began recording demos for original songs that Dylan initially envisioned other artists covering. These lo-fi recordings would be bootlegged for years before being released as *The Basement Tapes* in 1975.[2] An exploration of American roots, the recordings meandered through an abundance of traditional material. In his 1997 book, *Invisible Republic* (reprinted in paperback as *The Old Weird America* in 2001), rock-n-roll journalist Greil Marcus writes about Dylan's yearning for the undiscovered country of the past. These were songs of immortality, full of vegetables and death, as Dylan put it. They pointed back to a time when the King James Bible and the Farmer's Almanac were the only books in most homes, back when the emotive camp meetings of the

2. The reels were recorded between the time of Dylan's motorcycle crash and his recording of *John Wesley Harding* in 1968.

Second Great Awakening swept millennialism and revival across the countryside. In *Chronicles*, Dylan reminisces about the pervasive effect that folk music had on him at the level of consciousness:

> There was nothing easygoing about the folk songs I sang. They weren't friendly or ripe with mellowness. They didn't come gently to the shore. I guess you could say they weren't commercial. Not only that, my style was too erratic and hard to pigeonhole for the radio, and songs, to me, were more important than just light entertainment. They were my preceptor and guide into some altered consciousness of reality, some different republic, some liberated republic. Greil Marcus, the music historian, would some thirty years later call it "the invisible republic." (Dylan, 2004, 34–35)

Many of the songs he learned came from the *Anthology of American Folk Music* compiled by Harry Smith and issued by Folkways Records in 1952, although recorded a quarter-century earlier. Smith's compilation of eighty-four recordings across six LPs, accompanied by twenty-four pages of colorfully cryptic notes, had a significant effect on the young Dylan, who began listening to the LPs in 1959 and went on to record ten of the songs and rewrite two others by the end of 1961. Three of its songs are included on the two acoustic albums of cover music he recorded during the 1990s (*Good As I've Been to You* and *World Gone Wrong*), and many of its lyrics and melodies are blended into the original compositions that made up his 1997 album *Time Out of Mind*. But Harry Smith's anthology wasn't Dylan's only portal back to the American past. He explained to Mikal Gilmore in 2001 that Greil Marcus made too much of his creative indebtedness to the *Anthology of American Folk Music* and that he learned many traditional songs by hearing them performed live by legends like Clarence Ashley, Doc Watson, Dock Boggs, the Memphis Jug Band, and Furry Lewis.

He'd also heard a good deal of old-time music through the phonograph and over the AM radio growing up. In Scorsese's *No Direction Home* (2005), Dylan describes a significant memory from the age of ten when he discovered a turntable radio at his childhood home in Hibbing, characterizing it as an object with "mystical overtones." "There was a great big mahogany radio that had a 78 turntable when you opened up the top," he says. "And I hopped it up one day and there was a record on there, a country record, a song called 'Drifting Too Far from the Shore.' The sound of the record made me feel that I was somebody else, like I was maybe not even born to the right parents or something." The sound illuminated who he felt he was on a deeper level. Looking back on his youth at the age of fifty-six, he'd explain that his single-mindedness about music was a result of its having affected him at an early age in "a very very powerful way."

The spirit of the songs that he'd spend his life pursuing passed down universal parables of life, death, and regeneration. They beckoned him into a world of magical meanings where shape-shifting and immortality were possible. Dylan is quoted by Marcus as saying, "It comes from legends, Bibles, plagues, and it revolves around vegetables and death. There's nobody that's going to kill traditional music. All those songs about roses growing out of people's brains and lovers who are really geese and swans that turn into angels—they're not going to die" (Marcus, 2010, 113). Many quoted straight from the Bible, which had been a source of literary interest for Dylan since the year leading up to his bar mitzvah in Minnesota. In an interview with the writer Toby Thompson in 1968, Dylan's mother, Beatty, described visiting him during his eighteen-month hiatus from the public eye and seeing a Bible on a large stand in the middle of her son's Woodstock study. And his first official post-accident album, *John Wesley Harding* (1968), is bursting at the seams with Biblical allusions. The twelve spare and visionary songs on the album, which Dylan referred to as the first Biblical rock album, include more than sixty scriptural references across a series of sprawling narratives reminiscent of *The King James Bible*. The most well-known song off the album, "All Along the Watchtower," borrows images from Isaiah 28.

Fans were intrigued, if not somewhat puzzled, by what they heard on the Nashville-recorded album. This wasn't the Dylan of *Highway 61 Revisited* or *Blonde on Blonde*. People commented on the change in his voice. He sounded more melodic, reflective, and mature. When asked, he chalked up the change in his singing style to quitting smoking cigarettes and resisted discussing his objectives for the future. His purported goals were more immediate than long range—to live an ordinary life filled with family, fishing, hiking, and camping, and to get as much distance as possible from the "Bob Dylan" legend. Woodstock, for a time, was a place where he could live in peace and quiet, cultivating his own garden. But overzealous journalists and fans began terrorizing his family and dashed his hopes for anonymity.

"At one time the place had been a refuge, but now, no more," he laments in *Chronicles* of the years immediately following his accident. "Roadmaps to our homestead must have been posted in all fifty states for gangs of dropouts and druggies. Moochers showed up from as far away as California on pilgrimages. Goons were breaking into our place all hours of the night." He even caught a couple basking in a post-coital afterglow in his bed. His attempts to throw off this unwanted attention backfired. And to make matters worse, the press was continually promoting him as the mouthpiece of a generation. "My destiny lay down the road with whatever life invited, had nothing to do with representing any kind of civilization. Being true to yourself, that was the thing. I was more a cowpuncher than a Pied Piper."

The imperative to remain "true to yourself" seems to have led Dylan back to Nashville in 1969 to record a country western album, *Nashville Skyline*, with help from Johnny Cash, whom Dylan had met five years earlier at the 1964 Newport Folk Festival, at which Cash had given Dylan his guitar as a gesture of respect. With its steel pedal guitar, dobro, and cover photo of a sanguine-looking Dylan tipping his hat like a country squire on a Sunday outing, the sound, by his account, was closer to his "base" than *John Wesley Harding*. "These are the types of songs that I always felt like writing when I've been alone to do so," he explained to Wenner. "The songs reflect more of the inner me than the songs of the past." The ten songs on the album, which clocks in at a meager twenty-seven minutes, were reminiscent of the country tunes he'd heard over the radio growing up.

The compositions on his next record, the double LP *Self-Portrait* (1970), were actual covers of many of the songs he'd heard over the radio as a child and teenager. According to his Nashville producer Bob Johnston, Dylan showed up to the studio with "old books and Bibles" and just started recording. Al Kooper, who'd recorded with Dylan on *Blonde on Blonde*, playing the memorable organ riff on "Like a Rolling Stone," was surprised to find Dylan with a pile of *Sing Out!* magazines, picking out traditional songs like the Davis Sisters 1953 hit "I Forget More (Than You'll Ever Know)," "Let It Be Me," which had been popularized by The Everly Brothers, and "Blue Moon."

When he resumed the *Self-Portrait* sessions in New York that May, he shifted to folk songs that, like "Pretty Saro," reached back to eighteenth-century Scotland. Regardless of the album's commercial status (in his period review of *Self-Portrait*, Greil Marcus famously wrote in *Rolling Stone*, "What is this shit?"), and although Dylan would later distance himself from what he was trying to do, referring to it as a joke that he'd slapped together to fulfill his contractual obligations with Columbia, he ostensibly recorded many of the songs on the double album for deeply personal reasons. As he'd tell Jon Pareles of *The New York Times* in 1997 after recording two albums of traditional songs that drew from similar sources as the *Self-Portrait* sessions, "Those old songs are my lexicon and prayer book. All my beliefs come out of those songs." And one prominent belief in many of these songs—as with the original songs that they inspired Dylan to write—was that the self could be released from the prison house of the world.

During the recording of *The Basement Tapes* at Big Pink, members of The Band recall Dylan showing up with music and lyrics from folk songs popular during the Civil War and also with new songs that he'd been writing. They often didn't know which were the traditional songs and which were the originals because the compositions were so well blended. In his memoir, Garth Hudson recalls feeling this way about the song "I Shall Be Released," an original of Dylan's that The Band would end up recording on their 1968 debut album *Music from Big Pink*.

"I Shall Be Released"

Many of Dylan's classic songs over '65 and '66 have the feeling of T. S. Eliot's *The Waste Land*. If there's any lasting redemption to speak of on *Highway 61 Revisited* and *Blonde on Blonde*, it exists in the timbre and wail of a young singer transfiguring pathos, desire, and confusion into the catharsis of rhythm, lyric, and melody. The world in these songs is a heap of real and metaphorical rubble, a post-apocalyptic landscape of estrangement and danger. Although songs like "Visions of Johanna" and "I Want You" convey a fragile search for something genuine and whole, the yearning consistently falls short. Even the center of erotic love cannot hold for long beyond the blissful moment of consummation. The beleaguered singer of "Desolation Row" refuses to relate to an estranged lover whose Pollyannaish worldview cannot see the fragmentations and false appearances of the world. The song's final verse reads:

> Yes, I received your letter yesterday
> (About the time the doorknob broke)
> When you asked how I was doing
> Was that some kind of joke?
> All these people that you mention
> Yes, I know them, they're quite lame
> I had to rearrange their faces
> And give them all another name
> Right now I can't read too good
> Don't send me no more letters, no
> Not unless you mail them
> From Desolation Row

But then things changed. Allen Ginsberg once talked to Dylan about how his songwriting evolved after retreating to Woodstock. "In '68 [Dylan told] . . . me how he was writing shorter lines, with every line meaning something," Ginsberg reported in a period interview. "And from that time came some of the stuff . . . like 'I Shall Be Released' . . . There was to be no wasted language, no wasted breath." And line length wasn't the only change. From the time of *The Basement Tapes* on, the quality Dylan's search for meaning changed as well. It became less cynical and jaded, and more open to the possibility of transformation—vis-à-vis the realization of a deeper self or through union with a supreme power.

This is perhaps nowhere more evident than in the prison ballad "I Shall Be Released," a heart-wrenching song recorded at Big Pink in the summer of 1967. Whether it's mortality the singer yearns to be released from, the confining walls of a penitentiary, or the wounds of a sick soul, his trembling plea for release echoes the confusion, hope, and deep feeling of Dylan's life after his retreat:

> They say ev'ry man needs protection
> They say ev'ry man must fall
> Yet I swear I see my reflection
> Some place so high above this wall
> I see my light come shining
> From the west unto the east
> Any day now, any day now
> I shall be released

Seeing the light, of course, is a clichéd image of spiritual growth across the Judeo-Christian tradition—present, for example, in the story of Paul's conversion on the road to Damascus from Acts of the Apostles:

> As he neared Damascus on his journey, suddenly a light from heaven flashed around him. . . . The men traveling with Saul stood there speechless; they heard the sound but did not see anyone. Saul got up from the ground, but when he opened his eyes he could see nothing. So they led him by the hand into Damascus. For three days he was blind, and did not eat or drink anything. (Acts 9:3–9)

The light described in the song doesn't follow the east-to-west arc of the sun, but moves in the reverse from "the west unto the east." When the release comes, it will be like nothing the poet/singer has experienced up to that point. What it will amount to, and where it will lead, remain opened-ended questions. Robert Shelton puts it beautifully when he wrote the following of the song in *No Direction Home*: "Lyrics have a Biblical flow and serenity that swell toward each verse's line about ultimate release" (Shelton, 2010, 222). Later in his biography, he characterizes the song as a search for "personal salvation."

Unlike the bulk of the songs recorded at Big Pink, "I Shall Be Released" would remain a staple of Dylan's live repertoire. According to performance statistics posted as of April 2015 on Bob Dylan's official website, he has played the song live 491 times, first performing it in 1975 and last performing it in 2008. Heylin reports that it was a mainstay during Dylan's 115-date world tour across 1978, the second leg of which coincided with his Jesus experience and conversion to Christianity (to be addressed in the next chapter). Excluding the crowd-pleasing "All Along the Watchtower," which has been performed an estimated 2,252 times as of 2015, Dylan has performed "I Shall Be Released" more than any other song written and recorded in the two years following his motorcycle accident. The frequency of its inclusion on set lists suggests that the song has continued to mean something significant.

If songs from *The Basement Tapes* like "I Shall Be Released," "Tears of Rage," and the prescient "Sign on the Cross" signaled a redemptive hunger that impelled Dylan to explore "the old, weird America," the stripped down *John Wesley Harding* plunged him into the poetic depths of Jewish Scripture. The album features a bizarre assortment of gunslinger outlaws, western tricksters, immigrants, hoboes, drifters, and characters from Biblical parables, many on arduous journeys to discover purpose in a world gone terribly wrong. The memorable opening lines of "All Along the Watchtower" speak to an unfulfilled yearning, fear, and loathing that thread through the entire album: " 'There must be some way out of here', said the joker to the thief / 'There's too much confusion, I can't get no relief.' "

In *The Art of Biblical Narrative*, Robert Alter suggests that the repetition and "untidiness" of the narratives of Genesis and Exodus weren't merely a pre-modern editorial fluke (as many deconstructionists have suggested), but a purposeful attempt to encompass the dialectical tension between a divine plan and the "disorderly character of actual historical events," namely human freedom and the struggle to discern destiny. Alter calls this structure "composite artistry." Whether or not Dylan was aware of it, a look across the narratives of *John Wesley Harding* reveals a similar patchwork. And, much like the Jewish Bible, redemption in the album is realized through romantic love. The final two songs, "Down Along the Cove" and "I'll Be Your Baby Tonight," echo the lifesaving unions of Abraham and Sarah, Isaac and Rebekah—and Dylan's own real life safe haven in Sara and their growing family.

The two songs also foretell what was to come—*Nashville Skyline, Self-Portrait,* and *New Morning*, albums of bucolic contentment that, despite their mixed critical reception, were the songs of a man who temporarily hit the pay-dirt of a redemption that had a homespun, domestic quality straight out of the invisible republic.

Etiological Considerations

The British anthropologist Victor Turner's work on liminality (1964) provides a useful way of thinking about change across the life span. Turner provided a re-reading of Arnold van Gennep's understanding of rites of passage, with particular emphasis given to the transitional stage. Individuals at the thresholds of developmental transitions undergo experiences of disorientation and liminality followed by a process of "reintegration," with altered understandings of self, others, and world in accordance with new psychosocial roles. Turner showed how these "liminal" passages coincided with periods of socially validated transition. The "transitional-being" or "liminal *persona*" was observed in societies particularly during birth, puberty, marriage, sickness-into-health, old age, and death. Interestingly, the three quantum changes examined in this book coincide with times of developmental transition in Dylan's life.

The motorcycle crash was as transformative as it was not only because of the extent of Dylan's "injuries," but because the existential conditions of his life at the time were ripe for a seismic change. At least some of Dylan's experience of "in-between-ness" during the summer of 1966 can be chalked up to the fact that he was struggling to get off and/or recover from a cocktail of drugs that he'd relied on as "medicine" during the world tour.[3] There is ample documentary evidence of his having experimented with narcotics, psychedelics (marijuana and LSD), a range of uppers and downers, and copious amounts of alcohol.[4] When asked by *Playboy Magazine* about his relationship with illegal drugs in a 1966 interview Dylan responded, "I wouldn't advise anybody to use drugs—certainly not the hard drugs; drugs are medicine. But opium and hash and pot—now, these things aren't drugs; they just bend your mind a little. I think everybody's mind should be bent once in a while."

Rumors of heavier drug use (e.g., cocaine and heroin) have buzzed around Dylan for decades. A segment from a 1966 interview with Robert Shelton unearthed in 2011 reveals that Dylan had a $25-a-day heroin addiction in the early Sixties. "I got very, very strung out for a while," Dylan's voice can be heard saying. "I kicked the habit." Whether he did or not, and when, and how

3. In addition to amphetamines, John Lennon confirmed in a 1971 interview with *Rolling Stone* that he and Dylan had used heroin prior to shooting an outtake from *Eat the Document* in which the two men are driven around London in a limousine.

4. Alcohol seems to have been his substance of choice for much of the 1980s and 1990s.

often, is hard to tell. But his retreat to Woodstock in May 1966 included a serious attempt to get off the drugs he'd relied on while out on the road.

Psychologist Carlo DiClemente (1993) has written thoughtfully on addiction and personality change. According to his process theory, the movement from "addiction" to "cessation" often involves changes in behaviors, attitudes, and environments that can have a lasting impact on personality. The new self that is put forward during a sober period is susceptible to noticeable change in the event of a future relapse. As a result, the personality of a long-term addict can vacillate dramatically over time. Jefferson Singer (1997), a personality and clinical psychologist who has also published widely on addiction, studied how certain men suffering from chronic alcoholism weren't able to sustain continuity in their personal and professional lives. Devoid of a stable identity, they hover between boyhood and adulthood, trying on new identities and relationships. Nothing sticks for very long before it is replaced by something else.

A desire to sober up may have been one factor behind his change, but it wasn't the only factor. Celebrity itself added fuel to the imperative to change. It's important to keep in mind that Dylan became famous when he was in his early twenties. According to Erik Erikson's eight stages of psychosocial development (1959), the late teens and early twenties are the general period in the lifecycle when a consolidation of ego identity occurs. In *Chronicles*, Dylan suggests that he lacked a stable identity on the eve of his transformation into a national celebrity, writing, "I was lucky I had places to stay—even people who lived in New York sometimes didn't have one. There's a lot of things I didn't have, didn't have too much of a concrete identity either. 'I'm a rambler—I'm a gambler. I'm a long way from home.' That pretty much summed it up" (Dylan, 2004, 55). Dropping out of the limelight may have been a means of figuring out who he was on a deeper level. The sheer pace of his life had whisked him into the wiles of the world before he had time to establish an integrated sense of self.

Yet another factor behind his change was his marriage to Sara Lownds. At the time of their nuptials, "Like a Rolling Stone" had hit number one on the charts. He was at the peak of his commercial fame and enmeshed in an all-consuming world tour. At some point during this time, Dylan learned that Sara was pregnant with their first child, Jesse, who was born in New York on January 6, 1966. The experience of marriage and fatherhood began changing his way of thinking. "Having children changed my life and segregated me from just about everybody and everything that was going on," Dylan writes in *Chronicles*. "Outside of my family, nothing held any real interest for me and I was seeing everything through different glasses" (Dylan, 2004, 114).

Another considerable change occurred two years after the accident. Dylan's father, Abe, died of a heart attack in the spring of 1968 at the age of fifty-six. Abe's passing had a profound impact on Dylan. He'd stayed largely out of contact with his parents over the years leading up Abe's sudden death, not initially informing them of either his marriage or his accident. "I don't have a family," he reported in 1965. "I don't dislike them or anything, I just don't have contact with them." As a new father, he wanted to reach out to his own but couldn't. "Now there would be no way to say what I was never capable of saying before. . . ." Dylan writes of Abe in *Chronicles*. "The town he lived in and the town I lived in were not the same. All that aside, we had more in common now than ever—I, too, was a father three times over—there was a lot that I wanted to share, to tell him—and also now I was in a position to do a lot of things for him" (Dylan, 2004, 108).

Conclusion

Bob Dylan's breakdown and personal renewal across the second half of the 1960s makes sense against a backdrop of substance abuse, loss, and developmental transition. Faced with a dissolution of identity, he sought refuge in the progressive project of his life as a musician invested in "the old forms." Some people pray for guidance, others seek answers from therapists or clairvoyants. As Dylan would explain to Ron Rosenbaum in 1978, "Sometimes the world falls on your head, you know there are ways to get out, but you want to know which way. Usually there's someone who can tell you how to crawl out, which way to take." What he did was consult the annals of American musical tradition to determine who he was and where he was destined to travel next.

Dylan's descriptions of the accident and its aftermath over a period of nearly fifty years reveal a script that involves a loss of identity and purpose that leaves him vulnerable to death and destruction. The crisis is resolved through a reinvestment in the songs and artists of his youth, which help to grant him a renewed sense of purpose and self. The evolution of this script becomes increasingly theological in shape, theme, and nomenclature as time passes. This change reflects the pervasive influence of his next major change, a Born Again conversion experience in 1978. This experience incarnated the spirit of "the old forms" into the living reality of Jesus Christ. Although he has discussed this period of his life even less than his motorcycle accident, the descriptions he has offered reveal a middle-aged version of the destiny script reinscribed with overtly Christian symbols of death, rebirth, and personal salvation through a deep investment in Biblical tradition.

3 | SAVED

Only those who obey God's Law, consciously or not, will be
saved on judgment day.

—Romans

In 1974, a restless Bob Dylan roared out of a youthful retire-
ment and embarked on an extensive stadium tour with The
Band. According to his biographers, wanderlust got the better
of him while out on the road and he strayed from sobriety and
the predictable rhythms of domestic life. Rumors circulated that
his marriage was on the rocks. There were reports of copious one-
night stands and marital discord over a colossal copper-domed
home that the two were overseeing construction of in Carmel,
California.[1]

The Seventies were extraordinarily prolific years for Dylan
creatively, yet it seems that his attempts to balance an artistic life
with a domestic one were increasingly unsuccessful. The vivid

1. Restless and frustrated after a few years in Woodstock, Dylan changed things up by
moving back to Greenwich Village in 1970. Mobs continued to show up at his doorstep
on McDougal Street, prompting the Dylans to move out West, eventually settling in
California. A millionaire many times over, Dylan purchased and maintained a number
of properties during this time.

personalities, cinematic narratives, romantic intrigues, and bone-deep feelings that pervade the masterful album *Blood on the Tracks*, released in January 1975, paint the portrait of a complicated world of transient beauty, anguished loss, remorse, longing, and reinvention. The album's first song, the famous "Tangled Up in Blue," tells the convoluted story of a relationship across a cubist-influenced narrative that combines fictional and biographically accurate information that bears similarities to his courtship and marriage with Sara—in addition to language that mourns their struggles and tensions.

Many biographers have suggested that the larger album chronicled the gradual breakup of his marriage across the mid-Seventies. Even his youngest son, Jakob, who'd experience fame in the Nineties as the front man of his own rock band, The Wallflowers, commented that hearing the album was like listening to his parents talking.

According to Dylan's side of the story, his marriage to Sara became strained in April 1974 when he began taking painting lessons from a seventy-three-year-old Russian artist named Norman Raeben above Carnegie Hall in New York City. The lessons changed Dylan's way of thinking yet again. He is quoted as saying: "I went home after that first day and my wife never did understand me ever since that day. That's when our marriage started breaking up. She never knew what I was talking about, what I was thinking about. And I couldn't possibly explain it." Yet, in his usual fashion, Dylan dispelled any connection between *Blood on the Tracks* and his divorce, pointing out that the album was recorded a handful of years before his divorce and claiming that the primary source of inspiration for the album were the short stories of the Russian author Anton Chekov.

Dylan followed up on the commercial success of *Blood on the Tracks* just under a year later with another well-received album, *Desire.* Recorded in New York City over the course of a few hectic and inspired days, the album radiates with the pleasures and pains of earthly and divine forms of love. His complicated relationship to Sara, immortalized on the mystical song "Isis" and on the heart-wrenching and autobiographical final song, "Sara," haunts the album. Dylan seized upon the energy of the recording sessions by gathering together a troupe of Greenwich Village friends and performers and embarking upon a carnival-style tour of New England theaters and civic centers called the Rolling Thunder Revue. The star-studded entourage included Roger McGuinn, Joan Baez, Joni Mitchell, Ramblin' Jack Elliott, his poetic hero Allen Ginsberg, and, for a time, his very own mother, Beatty. He wore white-face makeup for no obvious reason, played doppelganger with Joan Baez on stage, and picked up the cause of the incarcerated boxer Rubin Carter as the raison d'etre of the tour. Carter, a middle-weight boxer from Patterson, New Jersey, had been convicted of a triple homicide in 1966. Dylan's song "Hurricane," co-written with the writer, psychoanalyst, and theater director, Jacque Levy, chronicled the racially motivated arrest and conviction of a man who could've been champion of the world.

Exonerating Carter wasn't the only objective of the tour. Dylan enlisted the help of playwright Sam Shepard to write and film a jumbled assortment of improvisational and scripted scenes featuring himself, Ronnie Hawkins, Sara Dylan, Joan Baez as the woman in white, Harry Dean Stanton, and the other Rolling

Thunder personalities acting out the ethereally convoluted romance of *Renaldo and Clara*.[2] Dylan's earnest attempts to explain the film in a heavy schedule of promotional interviews didn't help its commercial viability. "Its about the essence of man being alienated from himself and how, in order to free himself, to be reborn, he has to go outside himself. You can almost say that he dies in order to look at time and by strength of will can return to the same body," he said to *Playboy*'s Ron Rosenbaum in 1978. According to Dylan, the film was the most nakedly autobiographical piece of art he'd ever created. Unfortunately, his fans and followers also found it to be the most onerous to get through. Frustratingly abstract, it featured a character called "Dylan" played by Ronnie Hawkins, who wasn't supposed to be confused with the "real" Bob Dylan. And though Paul Williams and Allen Ginsberg have both written about it as brilliant and misunderstood, few people have clocked in all four hours.

Dylan decided to stage a comparatively less successful second leg of The Rolling Thunder Revue through the south in the spring of 1976 as a way of funding the mounting production costs of *Renaldo and Clara*. With Carter now exonerated, the tour lacked a unifying purpose and Dylan, preoccupied with an imploding marriage, was aloof and increasingly short-tempered. The second leg, which hit sparsely attended stadiums with a slightly altered retinue of musicians—dropping Ramblin' Jack Eliot, for instance, and picking up Stevie Wonder for a string of dates—was enervated compared to the smaller, indoor concerts of the previous fall.

2. Released in 1978 in three American cities, the four-hour long film was almost universally lampooned by critics and immediately pulled from distribution.

By the time the tour ended, Dylan began busying himself editing one hundred hours of *Ronaldo and Clara* footage with Howard Alk in Los Angeles. He and Sara had split for good. According to her divorce testimony, he'd brought a girlfriend to their home, and, when Sara confronted him the following morning at the kitchen table, he struck her across the face, injuring her jaw, and apparently ordering her to leave the house. His bizarre lifestyle, emotional cruelty, and chronic womanizing had gotten to be too much. A messy and tabloid-exploited legal battle complicated by a mutual demand for custody of their children was eventually settled on June 29, 1977, with Sara winning primary custody.

Dylan decided to recoup his financial losses by setting out on an ambitious and highly choreographed world tour allegedly in response to what ended up being a $10 million settlement. He leased commercial space in downtown Santa Monica and set up a headquarters where he could rehearse with his band, record music, store equipment, and sleep over if he was working late or needed privacy. Rundown Studios, as it was affectionately called, also had space for the musical and managerial employees he needed to keep his recording, tour, and publicity operations going on full throttle. A decision was made to work with Jerry Weintraub, Neil Diamond's tour manager, who helped Dylan enlist and manage a growing gaggle of musicians. This crew included a trio of Black female backup singers—Helena Springs, Jo Ann Harris, and Carolyn Dennis—and a horn section. The Vegas-style world tour commenced with a series of memorable concerts in Japan, recorded for the live album *Bob Dylan at Budokan* (released by Columbia on April 23, 1979).

When asked by Jonathan Cott why he was going out on the road again, Dylan shot back that it was all he knew how to do. "Ask Muhammad Ali why he fights one more fight," he suggested. "Go ask Marlon Brando why he makes one more movie. Ask Mick Jagger why he goes on the road. See what kind of answers you come up with. Is it so surprising I'm on the road? What else would I be doing in this life—meditating on the mountain? Whatever someone finds fulfilling, whatever his or her purpose is—that's all it is."

After the first leg of the tour ended, Dylan returned to Santa Monica and recorded a new album, the astrologically questing and propulsive *Street Legal*, which has long been criticized for its poor production quality and overreliance on backup singers and brassy horn chops. Although the tour had swept triumphantly through Japan, Australia, England, Germany, and France, it staggered once it reached home shores, and discouraging reviews of *Street Legal* cast a pall over the momentum. Dylan seemed frustrated and tired on stage and was no longer enjoying himself. According to this own reportage, he was also beleaguered by a lingering fever.

The majority of his biographers have suggested that the combined effects of his heartbreaking breakup, overwork, physical exhaustion, and the critical rejections of *Renaldo and Clara, Street Legal*, and the world tour in the American press took the proverbial wind from his sails and precipitated a full-blown crisis. In his short period book on Dylan's conversion to Christianity, *Dylan—What Happened?* (1980), rock-n-roll journalist Paul Williams paints the portrait of a man whose life was shattered by divorce. Williams suggests that Dylan was in desperate need of an eternal comforter and provider. All of the tricks that he was accustomed to using to buoy his spirits (e.g., the earthly trinity of wine, women, and song) had proved futile.

Much as it had before, his perennial fear of death was resurfacing. Howard Alk, who would end up committing suicide in 1982, suggested to Williams in 1980 that Dylan's "awareness of and fear of death" was a major factor in his conversion to Christianity. "As soon as Howard [Alk] spoke, I knew he was right . . ." Williams wrote in a 1988 essay entitled "Bob Dylan and Death." Central to this fear may have been the death of Elvis Presley. "In hindsight, and in light of comments Dylan has made since, Elvis Presley's death in August 1977 must have had a subtle but very powerful effect on Dylan, particularly in light of Elvis's age and the fact that Dylan in 1977 was 36 and closing fast on the big 40," Williams writes. "Forty is mid-life for a lot of us, but for one who identifies himself with other rock stars and culture heroes it can look like the end of the line." According to one of Dylan's girlfriend at the time, Faridi McFree, who was with him and his children at his farm in Minnesota when Elvis died (August 16, 1977), Dylan became morose and incommunicative for several days. The following year, he'd explain how news of Elvis' death struck him: "I went over my whole life," he reported. "I went over my whole childhood. I didn't talk to anyone for a week."

By the time the closing dates of the 1978 tour came around, Dylan was more than crestfallen and uninspired. He was chronically exhausted and physically ill, as he had been twelve years earlier in the spring of '66. On November 17, 1978, while playing a gig in San Diego, an audience member apparently threw a small silver cross onto the stage, and Dylan felt impelled to pick it up and put it into his pocket. The following night, in Tucson,

Arizona, he was feeling even worse and reached into his pocket, pulled out the cross, and put it on. That night, while stuck inside his hotel room, he apparently experienced the overwhelming presence of Jesus whose power and majesty he'd heard about through his girlfriends Helena Springs and Mary Alice Artes, in addition to his recently converted band mates Steven Soles, David Mansfield, and T-Bone Burrnett. It was Artes, though, who seems to have influenced him the most. She had recommitted herself to the Christianity of her youth through a Church in Tarzana, California, called the Vineyard Christian Fellowship, which Dylan soon joined. Founded by pastor Ken Gulliksen in 1974, it was a small but fast-growing evangelical church that emphasized redemption over judgment. Artes's recommitment impelled her to live a scripturally pure life by moving out on Dylan, with whom she was living at the time. Through her prompting, two Vineyard pastors, Larry Myers and Paul Emond, were dispatched to Dylan's home and ministered to him. He apparently received the Lord that day.

Although Dylan's new faith was a syncretistic amalgam that incorporated elements of the Jews-for-Jesus movement, Southern Californian New Age, and old fashion fire-and-brimstone millennialism, there was no doubt Jesus was smack dab in the middle of it. "Jesus did appear to me as King of Kings, and Lord of Lords . . .," he'd later explain. "I believe every knee shall bow one day, and He did die on the cross for all mankind."

Reflecting upon the significance of becoming Born Again three years after his encounter with Jesus in his Tucson hotel room, Dylan strained to explain the phenomenon in descriptive terms: "I mean it's like waking one day and can you imagine being reborn, can you imagine turning into another person? It's pretty scary if you think about it. . . . It happens spiritually, it don't happen mentally." And it hadn't only happened once. Although the Christological language that he began using in the late 1970s was new, the phenomenon of fundamental change underlying it wasn't. As he put it during an interview in 1985, "What I learned in Bible school was just . . . an extension of the same thing I believed in all along, but just couldn't verbalize or articulate."

One year after picking up the small silver cross from the floor of the stage while performing in November 1978, Dylan returned to San Diego with his gospel band in tow. During the concert, he opened up to the audience about his experience the previous year. In particular, he detailed his pre-conversion mental state with surprising candor:

> Towards the end of the show someone out in the crowd . . . knew I wasn't feeling too well. I think they could see that. And they threw a silver cross on the stage. Now usually I don't pick things up in front of the stage. . . . But I looked down at that cross. I said, "I gotta pick that up." So I picked up the cross and I put it in my pocket. . . . And I brought it backstage and I brought it with me to the next town, which was out in Arizona. . . . I was feeling even worse than I'd felt when I was in San Diego. I said, "Well, I need something tonight." I didn't know what it was. I was used to all kinds of things. I said, "I need something tonight that I didn't have before." And I looked in my pocket and I had this cross. (Dylan, 1979)

Six days after the Tucson show, while playing in Fort Worth, Texas, Dylan was spotted wearing the same cross around his neck. Although he wouldn't go public with his conversion for a number of months, concertgoers present during the final weeks of the '78 tour noticed that he'd replaced the lyrics from "Tangled Up in Blue" that referenced the song's mysterious lady quoting lines from a thirteenth-century poet with lines from the Gospel according to Matthew and then later from Jeremiah. By the time his next album, *Slow Train Coming*, was completed in the spring of 1979, stories of his conversion had trickled into the media. On May 22, at a pre-trial defamation-of-character deposition in Beverley Hills,[3] Dylan answered a question about his wealth by asking his own question, "You mean my treasure on earth?" And when asked who the fool was in the song, he wryly replied: "whoever Satan gave power to . . . whoever was blind to the truth and was living by his own truth." Several days later, the *Washington Post* broke the story of the rock star's conversion, quoting Dylan's pastor, Ken Gulliksen, who confirmed that the legend had indeed accepted Jesus as his personal savior.

The Script

As mentioned earlier, Silvan Tomkins (1995) thought that if a script were significantly amplified, it could shape one's interpretation of

3. Patty Valentine sued Dylan for use of her name in the song "Hurricane" off the 1976 album *Desire*.

future experiences. But static scripts were unlikely to endure over time. The lasting power of a script depended on its level of adaptive "plasticity." A plastic script is flexible enough to allow for revision, reordering, and the absorption of new scenes particular to the personal and contextual circumstances that trigger it. The disappearance of old scenes and the inclusion of new ones are revealing because they also help to illuminate that foundational structure that underlies the script and which is less likely to change. At the core of the destiny script, for instance, is a meta-narrative of death and redemptive change that found relatively easy expression in the Christian stories and symbols that Dylan embraced as he approached the age of forty.

January 1980

In late January 1980, Dylan's gospel tour played three nights at the Uptown Theater in Kansas City, Missouri. At some point during these shows, Paul Vitello, a young reporter for the *Kansas City Times*, managed to coax Dylan into discussing his conversion experience. The brief reflection Dylan shared was a perfect encapsulation of the destiny script. "Let's just say I had a knee-buckling experience," he explained. He then proceeded to touch upon the disenchantment of his life leading up to his encounter with Jesus. "Music wasn't like it used to be. We were filling halls, but I used to walk out on the street afterward and look up in the sky and know there was something else. . . . A lot of people have died along the way—the Janices and the Jimmys. . . . People get cynical, or comfortable in their own minds, and that makes you die too, but God has chosen to revive me." This description contains a familiar constellation of experiences. The sensation of feeling existentially adrift ("I used to walk out on the street afterward and look up in the sky and know there was something else") intensifies a vague but persistent threat of annihilation ("A lot of people have died along the way"), a threat that Dylan is redeemed from ("but God has chosen to revive me") through a wholehearted investment in "tradition"—in this case being Christianity—or more specifically, in the reality of Jesus, which Dylan substantiated by appealing to the Bible as a source of moral guidance and theological truth.

"People who believe in the coming of the Messiah live their lives right now, as if He was here," he'd explain in 1985. "That's my idea of it, anyway. I know people are going to say to themselves, 'What the fuck is this guy talking about?' but it's all there in black and white, the written and unwritten word. I don't have to defend this. The scriptures back me up."

May 1980

The first journalist to interview Dylan at length about his conversion was Karen Hughes, a writer for *The Dominion*, which was Wellington, New Zealand's daily newspaper. Unlike the off-the-cuff comments he made to Paul Vitello five months earlier, Dylan didn't say much to Hughes about his pre-conversion state of mind. Instead, he used vivid language to describe the rawness of the transformation. "Being born again is a hard thing," he said. "You ever seen a mother give birth to a child? Well it's painful. We don't like to lose those old attitudes and hang-ups."

The physical language he used to characterize the change was reminiscent of his description of his motorcycle crack-up twelve years earlier: "Jesus put his hand on me. It was a physical thing. I felt it. I felt it all over me. I felt my whole body tremble. The glory of the lord knocked me down and picked me up." Compare this language to the description he shared with Sam Shepard in *A Short Life of Trouble* (1987): "I went blind for a second and I kind of panicked or something, I stomped down on the brake and the rear wheel locked up on me and I went flyin'."

Another familiar trope that runs across both events is the new sense of self that the change gradually engenders. "Conversion takes time because you have to learn to crawl before you can walk," he told Hughes. "You have to learn to drink milk before you can eat meat. You're reborn, but like a baby. A baby doesn't know anything about this world and that's what it's like when you're reborn. You're a stranger. You have to learn all over again. God will show you what you need to know." It bears mentioning that much of this language is paraphrased from the Pauline Epistles, which Dylan quoted from fairly regularly following his conversion. In the third chapter of Paul's first letter to the Corinthians, Paul likens the wayward Corinthians to babies who must learn to drink milk before they can eat meat: "I have fed you with milk, and not with meat: for hitherto ye were not able to bear it, neither yet now are ye able" (1 Corinthians 3:2). Like many of the Born Again Christians studied by anthropologist Peter Stromberg in his book *Language and Self-Transformation* (1993), the canonical language of fundamentalist Christianity is grafted into the converts' self-expressions, thus inscribing their fears and hopes with new meanings. In Dylan's particular case, though, the canonical language of Christianity was joined to a preexisting schema of death and rebirth that can be traced back to his teenage years. The presence of a Messiah figure prompting the change was new, however.

Dylan alluded to a feeling of destiny behind Jesus' call:

> I guess He's always been calling me. . . . Of course, how would
> I have ever known that? That it was Jesus calling me. I always
> thought it was some voice that would be more identifiable.
> But Christ is calling everybody; we just turn him off. We just
> don't want to hear. We think he's gonna make our lives miser-
> able, you know what I mean. We think he's gonna make us do
> things we don't want to do. Or keep us from doing things we
> want to do.
>
> But God's got his own purpose and time for everything.
> He knew when I would respond to his call.

November 1980

The third and final time Dylan discussed his conversion with a journalist was in November 1980 with *The Los Angeles Times* music journalist Robert Hilburn. As he had with Karen Hughes, he discussed
the physicality of his experience in Tucson, describing a "vision and
feeling" that moved the hotel room and that "couldn't have been
anybody but Jesus." In an interesting revision that may have been a
conscious attempt to counteract the generally bad rap that his conversion had been receiving in the press, Dylan claimed that he was
neither "down and out," "miserable," nor "old and withering away"
leading up to his acceptance of Jesus, but, to the contrary, "relatively
content." However, his remarks on stage in San Diego in 1979, to
Paul Vitello in 1980, and the claims of his biographers, all paint a
somewhat bleaker portrait of his state of mind.

Through the prompting of "a very close friend" (again, pre-
sumably Mary Alice Artes), he accepted Jesus into his life—and

then, despite some initial resistance, attended most of a three-month Bible course at the Vineyard Christian Fellowship in Reseda, California, that changed his attitude toward the world. It was during this course that Dylan intensified his relationship to Biblical tradition. "I had always read the Bible," he explained, "but only looked at it as literature. I was never really instructed in it in a way that was meaningful to me." Much as he raided Harry Smith's *Anthology of American Folk Music* and other sources of American traditional music at Big Pink, he now searched through the Bible, earmarking pages, underlining key verses, and subsuming Biblical lingo into his song lyrics and everyday vernacular.

He took particular interest in the Book of Revelation, which seems to confirm Howard Alk's notion that death and destruction were indeed on his mind. When asked by Hilburn to assess whether his conversion made him feel or act differently, Dylan made an oblique reference to things that he was saying on stage between songs the previous year. "I was saying stuff I figured people needed to know. I thought I was giving people an idea of what was behind the songs." What he was doing was regaling his audiences with fire-and-brimstone prognostications that the end of history was fast approaching, which necessitated immediate repentance.

The brush with death that jolted him after his motorcycle accident in '66 had now morphed in scope, becoming more broadly social in focus. The feelings of estrangement and anxiety that rendered him susceptible to death were no longer specific to him, but plagued the entirety of America—and beyond! Accordingly, Dylan made a reference to the "sickness" of society to Hilburn. "When I walk around some of the towns we go, however, I'm totally convinced that people need Jesus," he said.

"Look at the junkies and the winos and the troubled people. It's all a sickness which can be healed in an instant. The powers that be won't let that happen. The powers that be say it has to be healed politically."

In the final question of the published interview, Hilburn asked Dylan whether music was still important to him. Once again, the answer that Dylan offered was saturated in the familiar theme of destiny:

> Music has given me a purpose. As a kid, there was rock. Later on, there was folk-blues music. It's not something that I just listen to as a passive person. It has always been in my blood and it has never failed me. Because of that, I'm disconnected from a lot of the pressures of life. It disconnects you from what people think about you. Attitudes don't really make too much difference when you can get on stage and play the guitar and sing songs. It's natural for me. I don't know why I was chosen to do it. I'm almost 40 now and I'm not tired of it yet.

The Progressive Project

The three-month Bible study that Dylan joined at the Vineyard Fellowship was on the topic of Discipleship and led by a young pastor named Bill Dwyer. During the study, attention was given to the Book of Revelation, which foretells the end of the world through a series of vivid scenes and numerically encoded allegories that exegetes have been speculating over for two millennia.

The course also introduced a receptive Dylan to Hal Lindsey's best-selling work *The Late Great Planet Earth* (1970), a book that interprets the allegories of Revelation through the lens of twentieth-century geopolitics. The millennial message behind Lindsay's calculations struck a familiar chord with Dylan, who had always held an apocalyptic view of the world (to be discussed further in Chapter 5). Lindsay's advice was to fulfill your God-given destiny before it was too late. There was simply no time to lose. Events in the world like the formation of Israel, the Soviet Union's ill-fated invasion of Afghanistan, and the Iranian Revolution pointed to a cataclysmic eventuality predicted by John of Patmos.

And so it wasn't long before a revitalized Dylan was back in the studio recording a new batch songs that he'd originally intended for Carolyn Dennis, one of several African American backup singers turned paramour—and, in Dennis's case, wife, and mother to Dylan's sixth child, Desiree (b. 1986). Yet instead of having her record them, he embraced his destiny and recorded them himself. Something about the compositions terrified him. "The songs that I wrote for *Slow Train* [frightened me]," Dylan would later admit. "I didn't like writing them. I didn't want to write them." But it was as if he had no choice. With some help from the young British pop guitarist and Dire Straits front man, Mark Knopfler, Dylan partnered with the famed soul producer Jerry Wexler at Muscle Shoals Studio in Sheffield, Alabama. Even though Wexler, Knopfler, and the other musicians were perplexed by the pointedly Christian nature of the songs, Dylan's faith was unflappable. He even tried interesting Jerry Wexler in the Good News, but was informed that he wouldn't make headway with "a sixty-two-year-old confirmed Jewish atheist."

Dylan surprised his fan base several months later by playing fourteen sold-out nights of his new Christian songs at San Francisco's Warfield Theatre. Some in the audience, like Paul Williams, were delighted, while others, such as *San Francisco Examiner* writer Philip Elwood, were appalled. The idea that the iconoclastic Bob Dylan, who'd been the voice of the Sixties counterculture, could accept the prepackaged doctrine of a narrow-minded fundamentalist church ruffled feathers. In his review published the next day, Elwood wrote: "90 straight minutes of poorly played, poorly presented and often poorly written songs . . . is a pretty grueling experience." Likewise, the *San Francisco Chronicle* reported "Dylan has written some of the most banal, uninspired and inventionless songs of his career for his Jesus phase."

Although he attracted a new audience of evangelical Christians, a group on the ascendency during the late 1970s and early 1980s, he alienated swaths of his secular liberal fan base with songs and onstage sermons that warned of end times and lambasted homosexuals and nonbelievers. At one show, he took on the City of San Francisco like Yahweh taking on the immorality of Sodom and Gomorrah:

> So now, you look around today, when started out this tour, we started out in San Francisco. It's a kind of unique town these days. I think it's either one-third or two-thirds of the population that are homosexuals in San Francisco. I've heard it said. Now, I guess they're working up to a hundred percent. I don't know. But anyway, it's a growing place for homosexuals, and

I read they have homosexual politics, and it's a political party.
I don't mean it's going on in somebody's closet, I mean it's po-
litical! All right, you know what I'm talking about? Anyway,
I would just think, well, I guess the iniquity's not yet full.
And I don't wanna be around when it is!

These mini sermons—collected and published in 1990 by
Hanuman Books as *Saved! The Gospel Speeches of Bob Dylan*—
suggest that his conversion was more than a passing musical fancy
or a desperate attempt to demythologize his own beleaguered
image. His post-conversion zeal hardened into righteousness as the
'79 tour made its way across the United States and Canada. But
apocalyptic predictions and moral judgments aside, the phenomenon underlying Dylan's Christianized persona was familiar: a
new musical identity and an accompanying cluster of life-defining
persuasions, perceptions, and values were linked to a musical tradition from his past, straight out of the Invisible Republic that
buzzed through his radio speakers growing up in Hibbing. It was
hardly the first time he'd delved into the Bible. As explored in the
previous chapter, he'd sought literary refuge in its proverbs and
parables during the writing and recording of *John Wesley Harding*
in 1968. Furthermore, during his youth in Hibbing, gospel music
coming in from the Grand Old Opry in Nashville, Tennessee, and
a thousand miles to the south from Shreveport, Louisiana, had
flooded him in a deluge of Biblical imagery.

It's also significant that his musical heroes had all recorded gospel
albums—from Johnny Cash to Elvis to Hank Williams. And at the
age of twelve, around the same period of time when he was preparing
for his bar mitzvah, he heard the legendary gospel group The Staples

Singers. Their sound was different, and the Biblical jeremiads and parables that thundered and moaned through their work riveted him, never entirely leaving his consciousness. "At midnight the gospel stuff would start," Dylan would later explain. "I got to be acquainted with the Swan Silvertones and the Dixie Hummingbirds, the Highway QC's and all that. But the Staple Singers came on . . . and they were so different" (in Marshall, 6). Before turning twenty, he performed Woody Guthrie's "Jesus Christ," and the traditional religious song "Jesus Met the Woman at the Well." And during his first year in New York, he attended Sunday gospel shows at the old Madison Square Garden and at the Apollo Theater in Harlem. Somewhere around this time, he composed a song that began and ended with a reference to the crucifixion, "Long Ago, Far Away." And his debut album, *Bob Dylan*, featured the heavily Christian "In My Time of Dyin'" and "Gospel Plow."

Whereas he'd borrowed from gospel as a young songwriter and scoured the Bible for its literary powers in 1968, his desperate need for truth at the age of thirty-seven necessitated a different sort of relationship to scripture. He wanted to push deeper, to touch the bone and nerve of what he referred to in 1985 as "the original rule." His exploration of this rule generated a new picture of who he was and what he'd been put on earth to accomplish. The more Bible he read and internalized, the more his sense of self changed. "You ask me about myself," Dylan said to Karen Hughes in the May 1980 interview quoted from earlier, "but I'm becoming less and less defined as Christ becomes more and more defined." And although this redefinition was predicated on what Dylan took to be Christ's living presence in the world, it was rooted in scripture. "It's HIM through YOU," he passionately explained. "'He's alive',

Paul said. 'I've been crucified with Christ, nevertheless I live. Yet not I but Christ who liveth in me.'"

Contrary to the notion that his Born Again period spanned only three years and then petered out, Dylan has never entirely disavowed the change that began taking root in the Tucson hotel room. Many years later, he would reveal to author Bill Flanagan that the spiritual laws of scripture continued to play a significant role in his songwriting, constituting a source of artistic and personal guidance that he returned to again and again. A similar sentiment was expressed to Mikal Gilmore in 1986, during the chaotic and disappointing *Knocked Out Loaded* recording sessions. When asked about the political principles that guided the songs of Springsteen and Mellencamp, Dylan was quoted as saying, "The only principles you can find are the principles in the Bible. . . . I hate to keep beating people over the head with the Bible, but that's the only instrument I know, the only thing that stays true." Like the eternal world of folk music, scriptural values were part of "the stuff that don't change."

In addition to the Book of Revelation, there were stories from the New Testament that Dylan repeatedly turned to as touchstones. One of these touchstones is the story of Gethsemane, which is the garden where Jesus goes at night after the last supper to contemplate his impending execution and where a small group of his disciples fall asleep despite being asked by Jesus to stay up with him. It's in the garden that Jesus clarifies his ultimate purpose.

"IN THE GARDEN"

The "personal salvation" for which Dylan yearned in "I Shall Be Released" came eleven years later when he encountered Jesus in the Tucson hotel room. The songs he wrote over the three years that followed are considered by some to be of the most vulnerable and impassioned of his career. And there was one song that Dylan himself seems to have felt particularly attached to: "In the Garden." Its first known performance was during his 1979 residency at the Warfield Theatre in San Francisco, and it officially appeared on *Saved* in 1980. From its initial performance in 1979 to its last (as of 2015) in 2002, Dylan's website indicates that it has been performed a total of 329 times, which, along with "Gotta Serve Somebody," "I Believe in You," and "Every Grain of Sand," make it among the most frequently performed songs from his gospel period. Over the two years that followed its debut, "In the Garden" quickly became the set closer for Dylan's live show.

In the liner notes of *Biograph* (released by Columbia Records in 1985 as a summary of his then nearly twenty-five-year recording career), Dylan wrote, "'In the Garden' is actually a classical piece; I don't know how in the world I wrote it but I was playing at the piano, closed my eyes and the chords just came to me." Twenty years later, he'd characterize his writing of "It's Alright, Ma" (1965) in a similar fashion to Ed Bradley: "Try to sit down and write something like that," he explained. "There's a magic to that, and it's not Siegfried and Roy kind of magic, you know? It's a different kind of a penetrating magic."

The magic that inspired "In the Garden" had a lasting effect on its creator. It remained a staple in his live show well into the late 1980s, years after he distanced himself from the Vineyard Fellowship and stopped evangelizing publically. In 1986, he opened his HBO *Hard to Handle* television special with the song, explaining to his live and television audience that it was "about my hero"— meaning Jesus. In 1988, he even lobbied Amnesty International to include the song on its fourteen-date world tour. Two years earlier, they'd chosen "I Shall Be Released" to conclude the final show, and in 1988, they'd selected "Chimes of Freedom." The evening before the tour came to an end, Dylan told a Pennsylvania audience that he wished Amnesty International would choose "In the Garden" for its tour the following year. It clearly meant something to him.

The song details the arrest of Jesus in the garden at Gethsemane as variously depicted across the synoptic gospels (Matthew, Mark, and Luke) and in the Gospel according to John, which Dylan drew from more than the other three when writing the lyrics. His version of the story consists of a series of rhetorical questions aimed at the doubters, disbelievers, and persecutors of Jesus— both in the Biblical world and the contemporary one. It has no chorus, just five verses of interrogatives, the first of which goes:

When they came for Him in the garden, did they know?
When they came for Him in the garden, did they know?
Did they know He was the Son of God, did they know that
    He was Lord?
Did they hear when He told Peter, "Peter, put up your sword"?
When they came for Him in the garden, did they know?
When they came for Him in the garden, did they know?

In *Still On the Road*, Clinton Heylin quotes an audio recording of Dylan introducing "In the Garden" at a November 1979 gig:

You know, when Jesus was in the Garden, [and] they came to get him, Peter, who was one of his men there with him . . .

took out his sword and he cut this man's ear off, when he came in to get Jesus, and Jesus says "Hold it Peter . . . Don't you think that if I pray to my father, he would give me twelve legions of angels to take care of this matter? This cup that's coming to me, I must drink it."

In the Gospel stories, as elsewhere in the Bible, "the cup" is a symbol for destiny. In addition to appearing in the gospel accounts of Gethsemane, the cup figures in Jewish wisdom literature. In Psalm 16, for example, the psalmist writes: "The Lord is my chosen portion / and my cup; / you hold my lot." It follows that drinking from "the cup" is a symbol for the fulfillment of destiny, hence Jesus' obligation to accept his arrest and execution as willed by God, despite the struggle it creates within the human part of his psyche. In Dylan's version, the events surrounding the night at Gethsemane are compressed into five versus concluding with the resurrection:

When He rose from the dead, did they believe?
When He rose from the dead, did they believe?
He said, "All power is given to Me in heaven and on earth"
Did they know right then and there what the power was worth?
When He rose from the dead, did they believe?
When He rose from the dead, did they believe?

Given the themes of personal death and rebirth that dominated Dylan's self-narrative at the time, it shouldn't be surprising that he'd express enthusiasm over a song that retold the story of Jesus' final stretch of hours. The physical pain of the crucifixion mirrors the pain of becoming born again. Recall, again, the visceral way that Dylan characterized his experience in the 1980 interview with Karen Hughes: "Jesus put his hand on me. It was a physical thing. I felt it all over me. I felt my whole body tremble. The glory of the Lord knocked me down and picked me up. Being born again is a hard thing. You ever seen a mother give birth to a child? Well it's painful. We don't like to lose those old attitudes and hang-ups." Interestingly, "In the Garden" is the only of Dylan's overtly Christian songs to include the term *born again*:

> When He spoke to them in the city, did they hear?
> When He spoke to them in the city, did they hear?
> Nicodemus came at night so he wouldn't be seen by men
> Saying, "Master, tell me why a man must be born again"
> When He spoke to them in the city, did they hear?
> When He spoke to them in the city, did they hear?

The combination of Dylan's celebrity and outspoken proselytizing during early gospel concerts turned his transformation into a public event; he wasn't hiding behind a mask. He'd lived through the struggles of his own garden of olives; accepted the cup of his destiny (as he came to understand it); was nailed onto a composite cross of fame, divorce, self-disgust, and early middle-age ennui; and was reborn. To quote again from his remarks to Paul Vitello in 1980, "A lot of people have died along the way—the Janices and the Jimmys. ... People get cynical, or comfortable in their own minds, and that makes you die too, but God has chosen to revive me." And even if his followers, fans, friends, and family refused to recognize the veracity of his new self, there was no doubt in his mind that he'd been revived and that Jesus Christ was why.

The fact that it remained the show-closing number from 1979 through 1981 suggests that, within the gospel set list, it held a place equivalent to "Like a Rolling Stone" or "All Along the Watchtower." Paul Williams writes emphatically about Dylan's performance of the song at the Theatre in *What Happened?*: "['In the Garden'] climaxes the show with a musical enactment of (what else?) scenes from the life of Christ (mostly based on the Gospel According to Saint John). . . . It all reaches back to the mystery plays of the middle ages, the religious dramas that are the starting point of modern theater. . . . This is rare, beautiful music, unlike anything Dylan or anyone else has done (though there might be faint traces of the *John Wesley Harding* album in there)." One gets the sense that Dylan experienced a feeling of completion when writing and performing the song. At least until things would change again, he may have temporarily reached what the poet Wallace Stevens describes as "a tower more precious than the view beyond."

Etiological Considerations

It's not surprising that Dylan's conversion occurred when it did. The entrance into middle age is a socially legitimized moment of transition that often leads to changes in values and perspectives, accompanied by rituals of symbolic death and renewal. Examples include reckonings that lead to new hobbies, commitments, life partnerships, values, and personal identities. The aftermath of

Dylan's motorcycle accident and conversion to Christianity both involved a movement from one life stage to another: in the former case, a protracted and capricious adolescence morphed into a comparatively sober and reflective adulthood via the experiences of marriage, fatherhood, a brush with mortality, and the passing of a father; in the latter, a combination of divorce, debauchery, and anxiety over death prompted a crisis of identity that was temporarily resolved through a conversion experience.

In his work on the psychology of religious conversion, Lewis Rambo (1993) developed a crisis model arguing that personal struggles and calamities often preceded conversion, which tended to follow a predictable sequence of stages that included a quest, an encounter, an interaction, a commitment, and future consequences. Rambo's fieldwork with subjects revealed crises of a varied sort, including mystical experiences, brushes with death, bodily sickness, significant loss, and disorienting sociocultural shifts. The conversion experience was a cognitive and affective means of managing and possibly resolving underlying discomfort and chaos.

The circumstances that surrounded Dylan's conversion follow Rambo's sequence nicely. According to Paul Williams (1980), again, the crisis of Dylan's divorce sent him on an existential quest for meaning outside the protective womb of his marriage and family. Psychological researchers interested in the topic of adult change have long identified divorce as a life-changing event capable of altering people at the level of identity (Josselson, 1996). Divorce can prompt questions and reappraisals of self, others, and world typical of a midlife crisis. "Dylan has always believed, not unreasonably, in the power of woman,"

Williams writes in *What Happened?* "When he finally lost faith in the ability of Women to save him (and he seems to have explored the matter very thoroughly, in and out of marriage, in the years 1974 through '78), his need for an alternative grew very great indeed, and he found what people in our culture most often find in the same circumstances: the uncritical hospitality of Jesus" (Williams, 1980, 16).

But prior to finding the "hospitality of Jesus," there was a period of intense searching, which is Rambo's second sequential stage. Williams and Shelton both commented on the questing quality that pulses through much of *Street Legal*, recorded months before his life-changing experience in Tucson. Shelton, for example, writes, "*Street-Legal* is one of Dylan's most overtly autobiographical albums, telling of loss, searching, estrangement, and exile. It also clearly foreshadows the Christian conversion ahead, but who among us could perceive it at that time? It is peopled by a group of narrators who are oppressed, wandering, and lonely, travelling in a foreign country of the spirit" (Shelton, 2010, 327).

Likewise, Clinton Heylin quotes Dylan as telling Philip Fleishman in a 1978 interview conducted during his world tour that: "The whole world is a prison. Life is a prison, we're all inside the body. . . . Only knowledge of yourself or the ultimate power can get you out of it. . . . Most people are working toward being one with God, trying to find him. They want to be one with the supreme power, they want to go Home, you know. From the minute they're born, they want to know what they're doing here."

Heylin also quotes Dylan's girlfriend through much of the '78 world tour, the young backup singer Helena Springs, about how Dylan was in a searching state of mind leading up to his conversion. "I think he was having some problems. . . . He called me and he asked me, and they were questions that no one could possibly help with. And I just said, 'Don't you ever pray?' . . . And he said, 'Pray?' Like that, you know. And he said, 'Really?' And he asked me more questions. . . . He started inquiring. . . . He's a very inquisitive person, which is one good thing about searching for truth" (Springs in Heylin, 2003, 493). Once again, Helena Springs wasn't the only person close to Dylan on the world tour who was a believing Christian. A core of other musicians in his traveling band, such as David Mansfield and Stephen Soles, in addition to T-Bone Burnett from Rolling Thunder Revue, had already been saved and were affiliated with the Vineyard Fellowship.

Dylan's pressing search for meaning on the cusp of midlife, coupled with his close proximity to an array of believing Christians, led to a precipitous immersion in the Vineyard Fellowship. At first he resisted the idea of a three-month Bible study, but a force he couldn't fully explain compelled him to attend. "I was sleeping one day and I just sat up in bed at seven in the morning and I was compelled to get dressed and drive over to the Bible school," he explained in 1980.

Conclusion

Arguably the biggest misinterpretation of Dylan popular lore is that the "gospel years" (1978–81) were an anomalous and embarrassing blip, a freaked-out fluke in the life of a celebrity musician desperate to drag an anchor—or, worse, a cynical ploy to open up a new market of listeners and concertgoers.[4] In his 2012 biography, *The Ballad of Bob Dylan*, Daniel Epstein writes disparagingly of what happened. "I had thought that, like Henry James, Dylan had a mind so fine that no idea could violate it. I was wrong. For the next two years he wrote and performed nothing but religious music, fire-and-brimstone gospel tunes of the most fundamental, doctrinaire, and judgmental ilk" (Epstein, 2012, 255). Epstein is hardly alone in reducing Dylan's religiosity to a period of two or three "god-awful" years. But such a reduction misses the strong religious impulse that has always been a defining part of his life. "I don't think I've ever been an agnostic," Dylan explained to Kurt Loder in 1984 when questioned about his religious identity. "I've always thought there's a superior power, that this is not the real world and that there's a world to come. That no soul has died, every soul is alive, either in holiness or in flames. And there's probably a lot of middle ground."

The truth is that Bob Dylan has always been on a quest for spiritual deliverance from the conditions of his life. The nineteenth-century French surrealist poet Arthur Rimbaud's notion "Je est un autre" ("I am someone else") was a lived reality for a young boy who survived the long brutal winters of northern Minnesota by staring out his bedroom window, allowing the lyrics and melodies from his radio to suggest a new sense of self that gave him purpose and safety amidst the air raid drills and death-related anxieties of the Cold War. Although the poetic language Dylan has used to explain the dialectic between death and rebirth has changed

4. Along these lines, Keith Richards referred to Dylan as "the prophet of profit" when he heard of his friend's conversion.

over the decades, the impulse to change had remained constant. A quick return to the three interviews (1969, 1987, and 2012) explored in Chapter 2 reveals a striking shift in nomenclature. The "real change" referred to in 1969 is referred to as a "transfiguration" forty-three years later. Another difference can be found in Dylan's need to find a "human" symbol to model his change after. Perhaps the old songs that led him to a deeper and more genuine expression of self after his motorcycle accident failed to offer enough of a defining self-picture at midlife. Clearly seeing "the picture you have in your mind of what you're about," as he put it to Ed Bradley in 2004, was now aided by the figure of Jesus, his hero. Always disposed to pull the mask off things, he looked deeply into the gospel traditions that had riveted him as a teenager and discovered that the Bible was the pillar and ground of what he'd heard coming out of the radio. As he explained to Karen Hughes, he was becoming less and less defined as Christ became more and more defined. With no clear father figure to model his masculinity after, he was a natural candidate to accept Jesus Christ as more than a God, but as an exemplar for who it was he was meant to be. Jesus would continue to factor into Dylan's spiritual and creative life ever after, appearing and reappearing in many of his songs, although never again mentioned by name. The eighth verse of "Red River Shore," an outtake from *Time Out of Mind* (1997), is a perfect example of Jesus' pervasive influence and presence in Dylan's world:

> Now I heard of a guy who lived a long time ago
> A man full of sorrow and strife
> That if someone around him died and was dead
> He knew how to bring 'em on back to life

What would change dramatically, however, were his feelings about organized religion. His spirituality morphed from a non-institutional form to an institutional one and then back again. Even in the heyday of his post-conversion zeal, Dylan expressed wariness over the politicization of Jesus by groups like the Moral Majority. And, according to Helena Springs, he was increasingly annoyed by the disapproving glances thrown his way by members of the Vineyard Fellowship after shows when he wanted to enjoy some wine backstage after a show. By the mid-1990s, after a period acquainting himself with the ultra-orthodox Chabad Lubavitch movement, he'd claim not adhering to "rabbis, preachers, [or] evangelists." Once again, it was in the Bible-smattered songs of his youth where he found his spirituality and guiding philosophy of life. Hence, the crisis of faith that threatened to end his career less than a decade after his conversion when the songs no longer worked.

4 | THE RECOMMITMENT

A musician must make music, an artist must paint, a poet
must write, if he is to be ultimately at peace with himself.
—Abraham Maslow

By the mid-Eighties Dylan had more or less stopped making
overtly Christian statements in public and had long since distanced himself from the Vineyard Fellowship. When asked about
his religious feelings during interviews his answers were opaque,
and he claimed the press had largely misunderstood his conversion. He noted he'd never actually said that he was "born again,"
at least not in the way many people seemed to think. His first post-
"gospel" album, the 1983 *Infidels*, enjoyed a spike of critical acclaim and temporarily stalled the downward trajectory of album
sales that had plagued *Saved* (1981) and *Shot of Love* (1982), both
of which had been criticized for being heavy on Jesus and light on
production quality.

On the heels of the reggae-infused and fan-pleasing *Infidels*,
though, came a series of less realized efforts. Aside from a
few standout songs (e.g., "Brownsville Girl," "Dark Eyes,"
and a rousing cover of the classic "Shenandoah"), *Empire
Burlesque* (1985), *Knocked Out Loaded* (1986), and *Down in the
Groove* (1988) were haphazardly recorded albums. None sold

particularly well, the records consisting of ragbag collections of halfhearted, shoddily produced material that fell short of previous work. An impatient Dylan, who preferred recording his albums with as few overdubs as possible in short, intense bursts of time, hadn't kept up with the technological innovations that revolutionized studio recording during the 1980s. His attempts to catch up by hiring backup bands comprised of younger punk and new wave musicians and collaborating with contemporary-minded producers like Arthur Baker fell short of keeping his atrophying brand up to date.

According to his biographers, his personal life was equally tumultuous through the majority of the decade. The womanizing that Sara indicated to friends had ended their marriage grew into a series of concurrent relationships with a host of women in an increasingly complicated financial, legal, and logistical shuffle of desire and desertion. Even his six-year second marriage to backup singer Carolyn Denis seems to have been motivated more by a commitment to provide for his sixth child, Desiree Gabrielle Dennis-Dylan (b. January 31, 1986), than a desire to settle down into a committed monogamous relationship like the one he had with Sara. He increasingly sought refuge from the complexity of his romantic entanglements by throwing himself into work.

Biographers like Howard Sounes (2011) claim that death was again in the air during the early to mid-1980s. He lost his musician friends John Lennon (d. 1980) to a psychotic assassin, Michael Bloomfield (d.1981) to heroin addiction, and his Christian composer Keith Green (d. 1982) to a plane crash. Most devastating of all, though, was the suicide of his friend, film collaborator, and neighbor Howard Alk (d. 1982). A stunned Dylan took a full two years off from touring and permanently shut down Rundown Studios, the location where the recently separated Alk had taken his own life by a heroin overdose sometime between New Year's Eve and New Year's Day 1982.

Overall, Dylan was lacking purpose, energy, and was no longer so invested in the art of live performance. The embarrassing debacle of *We Are the World*, his poorly amplified and atonal performance at *Live Aid* in 1984 (broadcast live to a television audience of an estimated two billion viewers), and his appearance in the flop of a film, *Hearts of Fire*, in 1987, revealed a middle-aged man at the nadir of a once great career that was quickly fizzling out. Like Elvis, a life of excess, celebrity, and prolific work had aged him beyond his linear years. His face was heavily creased and wrinkled from years of cigarette smoking, and his jagged teeth were yellowed by nicotine and neglect. At times, heavy drinking seemed to bloat his face and body; on other occasions, he had the gaunt, hungry appearance of a shifty cocaine addict. His kinky dark hair was styled into a pompadour/perm, and a long skinny earring dangled from his left earlobe. Dylan's sleeveless button down shirts, leather vests, and half gloves gave him to the look of an aging rock musician uncertain how to navigate a new era dominated by acts like Madonna, Michael Jackson, Duran Duran, and Prince.

"It's either your time or not your time," Dylan explained to Kurt Loder in 1984. "And I didn't feel like the last few years was really my time." And one year later, he'd tell *Rolling Stone*, "I've made all the difference I'm going to. My place is secure, whatever it is. I'm not worried about having to do the next thing or keeping in step with the times. I've sold millions of records. I've done all the big shows. I've had all the acclaim at one time or another. I'm not driven anymore to prove that I'm the top dog." In one interview, he explained that he could never write songs as good as the early ones again. He couldn't get back to that creative space if he tried.

In 1986, Toby Creswell of *Rolling Stone* (Australia) asked him if he felt guided to where he was. Dylan's answer exposed an unmistakable undercurrent of self-doubt: "You're always guided to where you are," he responded, "but you have the choice to mess it up. Sooner or later everything that goes around comes around. So, yeah, I feel like I've been guided to wherever it is I'm at right now, but I don't know whatever it is I'm supposed to be doing. I might have something else to do." A quarter of a century after he arrived in New York City, being "Bob Dylan" clearly had mixed dividends. Fame had forced him into living a spooky and paranoid lifestyle with few close friends and constant reminders of who he was when he was younger.

The following year, in 1987, a determined BBC film crew led by Christopher Sykes gained access to the legend for a one-to-one interview filmed for a documentary called *Getting to Dylan*. This interview captured a candid glimpse of the general disenchantment that enervated his life at the time. Conducted in his trailer while performing in Hamilton, Ontario, Dylan's ashen complexion and haggard demeanor suggested a level of exhaustion beyond a deficit of sleep. Before the interview got under way, he slipped out of his trailer and then returned with a telltale case of sniffles and wired eyes.

Sykes began by asking about a woman following him and claiming to be his sister. "There are people who follow me around and they have passports and they have drivers licenses and they all have Dylan as their name. What can I do about that? I can't do nothing about that," Dylan responded ruefully. Was he afraid of being hurt or killed by a psychopathic fan, as John Lennon had in 1980? His answer was *yes*. In fact, around the time of Lennon's assassination, a psychologically troubled fan named Carmel Hubbell, who had also taken to using the last name Dylan, had been stalking him relentlessly. She wrote him delusional letters, showed up at concerts, and compulsively phoned his Music Touring Company in Santa Monica. When Dylan went out on tour with his band, she showed up outside theaters and hotels demanding an audience, claiming that they had been lovers. She even broke into Rundown Studios on one occasion, harassing his staff, and began depositing leaflets on the windows of the studio and on the windshields of cars warning of "death devices." Worst of all, she rented a small house nearby Dylan's Point Dume estate and trespassed on his property nineteen times. After months of harassment, Los Angeles Superior Court granted a petition that kept Hubbell from stalking him.

During the Sykes interview, Dylan discussed the alienating consequences of fame in a way that hinted at the wreckage it had caused, especially in terms of interpersonal relationships. "People react to famous people, you know," he said. "So, if you talk to famous people, and I guess I'm one of them, because I have a certain degree of notoriety. . . . Fame, everybody just sort of copes with it in a different way. But nobody seems to think it's really what they were after. . . . It's like, say, you're passing a little pub or an inn, and you look through the window and see all the people eating and talking and carrying on. You can watch outside the window and you can see them all be very real with each other. As real as they're going to be, because when *you* walk into the room it's over. You won't see them being real anymore." One of Dylan's more affecting songs from this general period, "Dark Eyes," which appears on the uneven and ultra-Eighties-sounding *Empire Burlesque* (1985), conveys the alienation experienced by a performer who is simultaneously surrounded by thousands and by no one, and who spends his days in an unseen world where the dead rise:

> Oh, the gentlemen are talking and the midnight moon is on
>   the riverside
> They're drinking up and walking and it is time for me to slide
> I live in another world where life and death are memorized
> Where the earth is strung with lovers' pearls and all I see are
>   dark eyes

He was traveling from town to town, looking out drunkenly over sparsely attended venues and feeling increasingly isolated from other people and from his own dreams. Protective of his privacy and fearful for his safety, his life was devolving into an eccentric pattern of paranoia, addiction, work, and meaningless sex.

In what was likely an attempt to reinvigorate his dwindling base of listeners and fans, Dylan spent swaths of the later Eighties touring with Tom Petty and The Heartbreakers and also The Grateful Dead, with whom he played a short stadium tour in the summer of 1987. In preparation for The Dead shows, Dylan spent the month of June practicing with the band at their headquarters in San Rafael, California. The shows that followed were mixed at best by most estimates. Dylan often played songs in the wrong key and seemed to forget and/or mutter his own lyrics. A live album, *Dylan & The Dead*, was released, but critics received it poorly. *Rolling Stone* stated that the album "makes you wonder what the fuss was about," and *The Village Voice* wrote that what Dylan "makes of his catalogue here is exactly what he's been making of it for years—money."

The critics weren't the only ones down on what had become of Dylan's career. He was equally despondent about himself. "I'd seen all these titles written about me," Dylan reminisced to Ed Bradley in 2004. "I believed it, anyway. I wasn't getting any thrill out of performing. I thought it might be time to close it up . . . I had thought I'd just put it away for a while. But then I started thinking, 'That's enough, you know?'" Retiring from the music business looked like an increasingly necessary option. He'd lost his way from the philosophical identity that music had once provided him. One solution was to bury the loss in booze, and by many outside reports that's precisely what he did. But then it happened again: his destiny revealed itself.

The Script

Dylan has opened up on several occasions about a series of life-changing events that took place from June 1987 through the recording of his twenty-sixth studio album, *Oh Mercy*, in New Orleans from March through April 1989. His descriptions of what happened contain a reshuffled version of the destiny script. In June 1987, Dylan flew out to California to rehearse with The Grateful Dead. Much to his displeasure, he discovered that the band wanted to jam on songs that reached deeply into his back catalogue. "I had no feelings for any of those songs and didn't know how I could sing them with any intent," Dylan writes in *Chronicles*. "A lot of them might have been only sung once anyway, the time that they'd been recorded. There were so many that I couldn't tell which was which—I might even get the words to some mixed up with others" (Dylan, 2004, 149). But then something changed and, as he puts it, "everything just exploded."

September 1997

Dylan first spoke to a journalist about his third major turning point in a September 1997 interview with Stephen Gates, published in *Newsweek Magazine*. "I'd kind of reached the end of the line," he explained, lamenting the inauspicious place where he found himself in 1987. "Whatever I'd started out to do, it wasn't that. I was going to pack it in." But then, in early October after leaving The Dead tour to rejoin a subsequent leg of his world tour with Tom Petty, Dylan underwent a significant breakthrough that clarified his earthly purpose. "It's almost like I heard it as a voice," Dylan explained. "It wasn't like it was even me thinking it: 'I'm determined to stand, whether God will deliver me or not.'" According to Dylan, the shift was instantaneous, and his personal destiny was once again revealed: "And all of a sudden everything just exploded. It exploded every which way. And I noticed that all the people out there—I was used to them looking at the girl singers . . . I had them up there so I wouldn't feel so bad. But when that happened, nobody was looking at the girls anymore. They were looking at the main mike . . . I sort of knew—I've got to go out and play these songs. That's just what I must do."

November 2001

Four years later, Dylan talked to Mikal Gilmore of *Rolling Stone* about this turn in the road. After briefly touching upon the creative quagmire he found himself stuck in through the mid-Eighties, Gilmore asked about the "epiphany" that he had alluded to in the Gates interview. Dylan responded by describing two separate but related epiphanies: The first occurred at some point while he was playing with The Dead over the summer of 1987 and involved relearning how to play his old songs "using certain techniques that [he] had never thought about." These very techniques failed him, however, a few months later in Switzerland, forcing him to come up with another technique on the fly. "I was kind of standing on a different foundation at that point and realized, *'I could do this,'*" he explained enigmatically. "I found out I could do it effortlessly—that I could sing night after night after night and never get tired. I could project it out differently." Dylan's next statement shouldn't be the least bit surprising. He appeals to American musical tradition when trying to explain his newfound "technique." This time, though, it wasn't Harry Smith's *Anthology of American Folk Music* or the Bible that he cited. It's the blues-jazz player, Lonnie Johnson, who Dylan met and played with in New York in the mid-Sixties. Johnson was a prewar bluesman who enjoyed an unanticipated hit at the age of sixty with his recording of the 1939 song "Tomorrow Night," which Dylan covered on his 1992 collection of traditional folk songs and acoustic ballads, *Good As I Been to You*. As Dylan tells it, Johnson had taught him a guitar technique that "had to do with the mathematical order of the scale on a guitar," which he characterizes as "an ancient way of playing." Dylan then explains to Gilmore that he doesn't listen to many guitar players in "the rock & roll arena." He says, "...when I think of a guitar player, I think of somebody like Eddie Lang or Charlie Christian or Freddie Green." All three men were foundational American jazz swing guitarists who Dylan likely first heard over the radio as a child and adolescent.

When encouraged by Gilmore to talk about his "impassioned and affecting" performances of traditional folk music in concert, Dylan replies: "Folk music is where it all starts and in many ways ends. If you don't have that foundation, or if you're not knowledgeable about it and you don't know how to control that, and you don't feel historically tied to it, then what you're doing is not going to be as strong as it could be." As we have now seen on numerous occasions, having a "foundation" and being "historically tied" constitute much more than an aesthetic preference. It's a matter of psychological survival in a tumultuous world.

October 2004

Shortly after the release of Dylan's thirty-first studio album *Love and Theft* on the infamous date of September 11, 2001, Jeff Rosen, Dylan's longtime manager, announced that his boss had signed a four-book deal with Simon & Schuster. The first book would be a collection of memoirs. *Chronicles: Volume One* was published on October 4, 2004, to great critical acclaim. Although Dylan's novelistic approach took liberties with temporal sequences, fictionalized a host of facts, and appropriated a good deal of material from an array of literary sources, the work was remarkably accessible and accurate when read against the maddeningly experimental *Tarantula* (1971) or many of the fantastical yarns and digressions he had disseminated over the years to throw off the press.

Chronicles begins in New York City in the early Sixties, detailing Dylan's arrival into a snow-covered metropolis filled with colorful personalities, such as Dave Van Ronk and Izzy Young, and their youthful adventures around the folk clubs of Greenwich Village. Chapters two and three shift focus to his youth growing up in Hibbing, followed by the period of time after his motorcycle accident when he was attempting to distance himself from the "Bob Dylan" legend and raise his family in Woodstock. Chapter four, *Oh Mercy*, fast-forwards seventeen years and begins with a sustained reflection on his dispiriting tour with Tom Petty and The Heartbreakers.

"Always prolific but never exact, too many distractions had turned my musical path into a jungle of vines," Dylan writes. "I'd been following established customs and they weren't working. The windows had been boarded up for years and covered with cobwebs, and it's not like I didn't know it" (Dylan, 2004, 146). The previous decade, from his divorce through the late Eighties, had left him "whitewashed and wasted out professionally." Dylan writes: "Many times I'd come near the stage before a show and would catch myself thinking that I wasn't keeping my word with myself. What that word was, I couldn't exactly remember, but I knew it was back there somewhere" (Dylan, 2004, 147). He was plagued by a lack of identity, describing a "missing person" inside of himself. He'd become "a folk-rock relic, a wordsmith from bygone days, a fictitious head of state from a place nobody knows"—living "in the bottomless pit of cultural oblivion" (Dylan, 2004, 147).

Bewildered by The Dead's request to rehearse material from his back catalogue, Dylan describes bolting from an early rehearsal and walking down a drizzly street in San Rafael for several blocks until he passed a tiny bar from which he heard live jazz being performed. He stepped in, ordered a gin and tonic, and stood listening to the trio from the empty bar. His attention was immediately drawn to the singer—"An older man, he wore a mohair suit, flat cap with a little brim and had a shiny necktie" (Dylan, 2004, 150). The singer reminded him of Billy Eckstine, a black American singer and bandleader of the swing era who Dylan first heard growing up. The subtle power of the singer's voice suggested a mysterious new source of power. Once again, the musical traditions that crackled out from his childhood radio were there to guide him forward.

The language of self-discovery that Dylan uses to describe the epiphany he experienced in the tiny bar is redemptive in theme and tone: "Suddenly and without warning, it was like the guy had an open window to my soul. . . . I could feel how he worked at getting his power, what he was doing to get at it. I knew where the power was coming from and it wasn't his voice, though the voice brought me sharply back to myself. I used to do this thing, I'm thinking. It was a long time ago and it had been automatic" (150–151). Awakened by the old jazz singer's example, he returned to The Dead's rehearsal hall ready to put what he learned to immediate work. According to his appraisal, the breakthrough had religious overtones. "It was like parts of my psyche were being communicated to by angels. There was a big fire in the fireplace and the wind was making it roar. The veil had lifted" (146).

This cluster of scenes is juxtaposed with a cluster of similar scenes that took place several months later. After his shows with The Dead came to an end in late July 1987, Dylan returned to the

Petty tour revitalized and confident of his fate as a musical troubadour whose destiny it was to write and perform to the best of
his ability. But then while performing in Switzerland, he hit the
creative block alluded to in the 1997 and 2001 interviews quoted
from earlier. Dylan writes about how he was forced to jump-start
the techniques on the fly. "I just did it automatically out of thin
air, cast my own spell to drive out the devil. Instantly, it was like
a thoroughbred had charged through the gates. Everything came
back, and it came back in multi-dimension. Even I was surprised.
It left me kind of shaky. Immediately, I was flying high. This new
thing had taken place right in front of everybody's eyes. A difference in energy might have been perceived, but that was about
all. Nobody would have noticed that a metamorphosis had taken
place" (153). This intensification of the change that began in San
Raphael charged him with a renewed sense of purpose. "If I ever
wanted a different purpose, I had one. It was like I'd become a new
performer, an unknown one in the true sense of the word."

Although he took the advice of his manager, Elliot Roberts,
and consented to a several-month hiatus after the tour with Tom
Petty and The Heartbreakers concluded, he eagerly anticipated
the spring of 1988, which was when he planned to hit the road
for a three-year schedule in which he'd play the same towns and
cities each year as a way of gradually attracting a new fan base.
"Spring seemed like a long time to wait, but I can be patient,"
writes Dylan. "There were plenty of days coming when it would
all come together. My destiny was shining silver in the sun."

But then a freak accident mangled his arm and hand terribly. The source of this mysterious accident is conspicuously
absent from *Chronicles*. Manipulating chronology for maximum

dramatic effect, Dylan begins the "Oh Mercy" chapter with mention of the injury: "It was 1987 and my hand, which had been ungodly injured in a freak accident, was in a state of regeneration. It had been ripped and mangled to the bone and was still in the acute stage—it didn't even feel like it was mine." Uncertain whether he'd be able to continue performing, he spiraled into a sustained depression during which he considered hanging it up and retiring. He writes of being back at square one, or worse. "Returning from the emergency room with my arm entombed in plaster I fell into a chair—something heavy had come against me. It was like a black leopard had torn into my flesh" (156).

However, the guitar playing technique taught to him by Lonnie Johnson helped rehabilitate his hand. As mentioned before, Lonnie Johnson, who also imparted his musical technique to the delta blues great Robert Johnson, taught Dylan a cryptic and mathematical style of guitar playing in the early Sixties during the folk revival in New York City. Dylan claims not having understood its significance at the time, but suddenly, two-and-a-half decades later, Johnson's "mysterious system of triplets" was revitalizing his world. As he had in the 1997 interview with Stephen Gates, Dylan contextualizes this way of playing within American musical tradition. Slowly healing at home in the company of his family (including his mother and aunt for a period of time), he began writing songs again. On the advice of U2's Bono, who was visiting for a spell, Dylan decided to travel down to New Orleans to record his most realized album of the late-Eighties, *Oh Mercy*, with the innovative producer Daniel Lanois, a decision which he likens in *Chronicles* to "something foretold in the scriptures" (179).

The Progressive Project

Oh Mercy was recorded in a five-story house in Uptown New Orleans that Lanois rented for Dylan and a group of local musicians capable of creating the "Louisiana swamp sound." Setting up the musicians in a horseshoe around his soundboard, Lanois set to work, pushing the occasionally petulant Dylan to record a collection of songs worthy of his name and talent. Although frustrated with the recording process and at frequent loggerheads with Lanois himself, Dylan was intent on creating something of merit. In *Chronicles*, he juxtaposes the ups and downs of the sessions with his nonworking hours in and around New Orleans, a city he describes as "one very long poem." The Audubon Place house he and Carolyn Dennis were staying at was located near the studio and offered him a much-needed refuge from the pressures of recording.

In an exquisitely written section of the memoir, Dylan reflects upon the radio that was always on in the kitchen of the house, broadcasting a particular station, WWOZ. The station had a nighttime DJ named Brown Sugar who played "all the greats" from Dylan's youth—Wynonie Harris, Roy Brown, Ivory Joe Hunter, Little Walter, Lightnin' Hopkins, and Chuck Willis. Dylan writes about how Brown Sugar's "thick, slow, dreamy, oozing molasses voice" filled him with "inner peace and serenity," easing the frustration that had been complicating his attempts at making the record with Lanois.

"WWOZ was the kind of station I used to listen to late at night growing up, and it brought me back to the trials of my youth and touched the spirit of it," Dylan writes. "Back then when something was wrong the radio could lay hands on you and you'd be all right. There was a country station, too, that came on early, before daylight, that played all the '50s songs, a lot of Western Swing stuff . . . I listened to that a lot. There had been a station like that also broadcast into my hometown (Hibbing)." Something about listening to these stations gave Dylan a feeling of new beginnings not unlike ones he'd felt at key moments earlier in his life. "In a weird sense," he writes, "I felt like I was starting over, beginning to live my life again." Much as it had in the aftermath of his motorcycle accident, the sonic salvation of traditional music was there to help. Jesus may have laid his hands on Dylan in the Tucson hotel room in the late Seventies, but the radio had apparently been doing the same for years.

After recounting the radio's healing powers, Dylan pinpoints the moment when his work on the album began to find traction. Stymied by several disappointing hours trying to get down the outtake "Dignity," he had a breakthrough on a new song he'd written called "Where Teardrops Fall." Recorded, according to Dylan, in a few minutes without a substantial rehearsal, the song concluded with "a sobbing solo" on saxophone that Dylan reports nearly took his breath away. Here's how he describes his response in *Chronicles*:

> I leaned over and caught a glimpse of the musician's face. He'd been sitting there the whole night in the dark and I hadn't noticed him. The man was the spitting image of Blind Gary Davis, the singing reverend that I'd known and followed around years earlier. What was he doing here?

Same guy, same checks and chin, fedora, dark glasses. Same
build, same height, same long black coat—the works. It was
eerie. (191)

Blind Gary Davis was an influential figure in Dylan's artistic
development. He was born in South Carolina in 1896. Black,
blind, and poor, Davis learned to play guitar after hearing someone playing a primitive form of the blues. According to Davis's
rather mystical telling of it, a mysterious blues guitarist and singer
named Porter Davis drifted through his hometown one day and
performed, playing the song "Delia," which Davis later subsumed
into his own repertoire, and which Dylan recorded in 1960 and
then again in 1993 on his second consecutive collection of traditional folk songs, *World Gone Wrong*.

Davis migrated north to Durham, North Carolina, where
he played the blues and was recorded by the American Record
Company. In 1937, he converted to Christianity and was later
ordained a Baptist minister. For a period of time after his conversion, he preferred to play gospel music over the profane blues that
had helped him make a name for himself. With the blues scene
around Durham on the decline, Davis headed north to New York
City where he lived, played, and was eventually "rediscovered"
during the folk revival of the early Sixties, even performing at
The Newport Folk Festival. A steady stream of younger white
musicians, including Dave Van Ronk and Bob Dylan, befriended
Davis and were informally mentored by him. Imagining the New
Orleans saxophonist as Davis reincarnate (he died from a heart
attack in 1972), Dylan felt reaffirmed in his purpose: "He peered
across the room at me in an odd way, like he had the ability to

see beyond the moment, like he'd thrown a rope line out to grip. All of a sudden I know that I'm in the right place doing the right thing at the right time and Lanois is the right cat. Felt like I had turned a corner and was seeing the sight of a god's face" (Dylan, 2004, 191).

Dylan had been greatly inspired when he heard Davis perform live in the early Sixties at Gerde's Folk City, which, under the management of Mike Porco, booked Gary Davis along with other greats like Cisco Houston. Addressing the inspiration behind *World Gone Wrong* in a 1993 interview with Gary Hill published in the fan magazine *ISIS*, Dylan referenced the influence that Davis and other blues greats had had on him. "These people who originated this music, they're all Shakespeares, you know? . . . There was a bunch of us, me included, who got to see all these people close up, people like Son House, Reverend Gary Davis, or Sleepy John Estes. . . . Those vibes will carry into you forever, really, so it's like those people, they're still here to me. They're not ghosts of the past or anything. They're continually there."

Part of the reason that the songs for *Oh Mercy* came naturally was because Dylan was finding his way back to his base, as he'd done decades earlier at Big Pink. The living "ghosts" of Reverend Gary Davis, Hank Williams, and all the "early rhythm-and-blues and rural Southern gospel music" he heard on the radio in Hibbing and on WWOZ while in New Orleans helped guide him. Whereas his deepening into tradition had consisted of covering traditional music as a young man and then investing himself in Jesus and the Bible at middle age, when nearing the age of fifty, he appealed directly to the originators of "those old songs," whose descriptions possess a messianic quality reminiscent of the

language he once used to describe his encounter with and understanding of Jesus.

Dylan's musical pantheon has always been broad, encompassing different types of American folk traditions. As he'd explain to
The New York Times in 1997, "My songs come out of folk music.
I love that whole pantheon. To me there's no difference between
Muddy Waters and Bill Monroe." One of the founding fathers
of bluegrass music, Bill Monroe (1909–96), was born in Rosine,
Kentucky. Monroe played along with Earl Scruggs, creating and
promulgating bluegrass across the southern and midwestern parts
of America. In a *Rolling Stone* interview with Kurt Lodder, Dylan
mentioned Monroe's ongoing influence on him: "The stuff that
I grew up on never grows old. I was just fortunate enough to get it
and understand it at that early age, and it still rings true for me. . . .
I'd still rather listen to Bill and Charlie Monroe than any current
record. That's what America's all about to me. I mean, they don't
have to make any more new records—there's enough old ones,
you know?"

Muddy Waters (1913–83) was born along the banks of Deer
Creek, which flows south through the Mississippi delta. Waters
was one of Dylan's many Delta blues heroes. Guitars in hand, they
wandered like Robert Johnson to the crossroads at midnight,
rode boxcars across America, plucked out spirituals at Christian
camp meetings, and eventually migrated to industrialized and
overcrowded cities such as Chicago and Detroit to play the blues.
Some disappeared into obscurity, while others, like Lead Belly,
was found in a Louisiana penitentiary. Over time, many of these
bluesmen were "rediscovered" by eager white audiences led by ethnomusicologists like Harry Smith, Charles Seeger, and Jon and

Alan Lomax. For performers like Reverend Gary Davis, Lead Belly, and Lonnie Johnson, these "rediscoveries" prompted later-life revivals geared toward the liberal white hootenanny folk scene that young college-aged kids like Bob Dylan found himself enthralled by—so much so in his case that he appropriated a Delta blues identity as his own. Monroe and Waters, and Johnny Cash for that matter, were something that Dylan could never himself be. They were from a different place and time and felt closer to the roots of American folk traditions.

It's likely no coincidence that Dylan traveled to New Orleans when trying to reconnect with his creative source as a fifty-year-old man. After all, it had been a mecca on his cultural map since his days listening to the airwaves out of Shreveport, Louisiana. In *Chronicles*, Dylan reminds his readers that Highway 61 and the mighty Mississippi River both start up in northern Minnesota. Although New Orleans itself was not the cradle of the Delta blues, its geographical position straddling the Mississippi River made it a hub for jazz, early rhythm-and-blues, Cajun music, and a host of influences from the Caribbean. When Dylan visited New Orleans to meet Lanois and hear outtakes from the album he was then producing for the Neville Brothers, he decided he wanted to make a record there.

Dylan has explicitly attached the archipelago of memories explored in this chapter—from the experience in San Rafael rehearsing with The Grateful Dead to the experience of recording *Oh Mercy*—to a renewed sense of purpose and energy that impelled the so-called never-ending tour, which commenced in June 1988 and continues through the time of the composition of this book. Dylan was reminded of *who* he was and *what* he was called to do. He decided to devote the rest of his life to the work of being a troubadour, no matter the toll on his personal life and physical health. And, according to Heylin and Sounes, from the late Eighties through the early Nineties, his life was in an ongoing state of turmoil. He was purportedly drinking heavily and distracted by a complicated web of short- and long-term sexual affairs. But he continued touring—year after year—molding a traveling band led by bassist Tony Garnier that didn't quit. But, regardless of the state of his personal affairs, Dylan's commercial successes in the mid-to-late Nineties and on into the new millennium transformed his touring company into a highly lucrative venture.

When asked by Ed Bradley why he was still out there touring year after year, Dylan answered: "It goes back to that destiny thing. I mean, I made a bargain with it, you know, long time ago. And I'm holding up my end . . . to get where I am now." And with whom exactly did he make the bargain, inquired Bradley. "With the chief commander," replied Dylan, smiling. "In this earth and in the world we can't see." Dylan's bargain with the "chief commander" required that he follow his sense of purpose to the bitter end.

"WHERE TEARDROPS FALL"

Clinton Heylin expresses puzzlement over why Dylan spends time in *Chronicles* detailing his experience recording "Where Teardrops Fall," the track on *Oh Mercy* described in the previous section. In *Still On the Road*, Heylin refers to it as a "piece of fluff" that Dylan wasted time on. Whereas most of the songs on *Oh Mercy* are given a quick gloss in *Chronicles*, Dylan spends several impassioned paragraphs recounting his late-night recording of the song, which, as mentioned earlier, he characterizes as the breakthrough he'd traveled to New Orleans hoping for. Heylin uses the logbooks of the actual recording sessions to debunk the fiction of a single late-night session, revealing that Dylan actually spent several days painstakingly recording and overdubbing until it was done. From a psychological perspective, though, the historical inaccuracy of Dylan's version is of less interest than what the "fictionalized" memory reveals about his deeply personal relationship to the song.

Dylan, who once remarked to a friend that he rarely got out of bed without reading ten chapters from the Bible, had the scriptures on his mind in New Orleans. As Scott Marshall and others have noted, the ten songs on *Oh Mercy* are teeming with Biblical references and quotations, so much so that Marshall refers to it as a companion piece to the uber-Christian *Slow Train Coming* recorded a decade earlier. Anyone familiar with the New Testament might recognize images from "Where Teardrops Fall" as more than a love song. Modeled after the Psalms (in which David addresses Yahweh in the second person), the song conjures the Place of the Skull, or Golgotha (referred to as Calvary in the King James Bible). This was the location immediately outside Jerusalem where Jesus and two thieves were crucified. Golgotha was where Jesus fulfilled his ultimate destiny by undergoing a final transfiguration from body to spirit. Whereas he accepts the cup of his fate at Gethsemane, he drains it at Golgotha.

The poet/singer internalizes the story of the crucifixion to such a degree that he lives out a parallel experience in which he is both observer and subject. Teardrops, which are frequently symbolic of spiritual struggle and growth, fall at Golgotha (with Jesus crying out "*Eli, Eli, lema sabachthani?*"[1]), much as they do in the song. Additionally, like the desolate place described in the song ("far away and over the wall"), the Biblical Golgotha is described by Paul (Hebrews 13:12) and in the Gospel according to John (John 19:20) as located outside the walls of Jerusalem, a fact that has been confirmed by Biblical historians like Helmut Koester. Other similarities exist as well:

> "Far away in the stormy night / Far away and over the wall / You are there in the flickering light / Where teardrops fall"
>> *It was about twelve o'clock when the sun stopped shining and darkness covered the whole country until three o'clock. (Luke 23: 44–45)*

> "I've torn my clothes and I've drained the cup / Strippin' away at it all"
>> *Then they crucified him and divided his clothes among themselves . . . (Matthew 15:24)*

Far from merely the retelling of a Golgotha-inspired story, Dylan overlays the third verse with particulars from his own life at the time, especially his struggle to reconnect with his God-given purpose as a songwriter and performer:

> We banged the drum slowly
> And played the fife lowly

---

1. Famously translated from the Aramaic as: *My God, my God, why have you forsaken me?*

> You know the song in my heart
> In the turning of twilight
> In the shadows of moonlight
> You can show me a new place to start

Compare these lyrics to Dylan's memories from *Chronicles*— "At about three in the morning we had played ourselves out and just started playing any old stuff. . . . In the midst of all this, I played another new song I had written, 'Where Teardrops Fall.' I showed it quickly to Dopsie and we recorded it. It took about five minutes and it wasn't rehearsed . . . All of the sudden I know that I'm in the right place doing the right thing at the right time and Lanois is the right cat. Felt like I had turned the corner. . . ." (191). Supposing that Clinton Heylin's debunking of Dylan's story about recording "Where Teardrops Fall" is accurate, it's possible that the song and its lyrics shaped Dylan's memory of the experience into an especially redemptive form.

* * *

When read together, "I Shall Be Released" (from Chapter 2), "In the Garden" (from Chapter 3), and "Where Teardrops Fall" tell a story that parallels Bob Dylan's own spiritual evolution. The post-accident yearning captured by "I Shall Be Released" blossomed a decade later into a full-blown religious conversion—which morphed over time from the zealous proclamations of a recent convert closing his shows with "In the Garden" to the humble depths of a fifty-year-old man recording "Where Teardrops Fall" in New Orleans.

The narrative suggested by these songs conveys a Biblically patterned progression from the Babylonian Exile to Gethsemane to Golgotha predicated on a cycle of struggle, death, and subsequent rebirth. The forms of religious yearning and change present across the songs reflect a defining feature of much of Christian spirituality—that is, it's progressive (as opposed to regressive) nature. According to theologians like Bruce Chilton, transfiguration isn't a one-shot deal, but an ongoing process of self-transformation. Within Late Antique and Medieval Christianity, transfiguration was a popular theological concept. It was widely believed that the bodies and spirits of certain people—namely saints—were perennially "transformed into the power of God, and [...] kindled into fire and light," to quote from the fourth century *Homilies of Saint Macarius*. T. S. Eliot's *Four Quartets,* easily one of the most profound modern meditations on Christian spirituality, conveys this perspective poetically in section V of "East Coker":

> Old men ought to be explorers
> Here and there does not matter
> We must be still and still moving
> Into another intensity
> For a further union, a deeper communion
> Through the dark cold and empty desolation,
> The wave cry, the wind cry, the vast waters
> Of the petrel and the porpoise. In my end is my beginning.

Just as Jesus himself (especially in the Gospel according to Mark) undergoes several transfigurations—from his baptism in the River Jordan, to his transfiguration in front of his disciples, to his death on the cross at Golgotha—people of faith follow their senses of God's presence over the stretches of their lives, continually becoming, yearning for what the Catholic theologian Karl Rahner has referred to as "a forever-receding horizon." Along these lines, it's interesting that the lyrics to "Where Teardrops Fall" undergo a tense shift in the final verse to conclude on a note of futurity:

> Roses are red, violets are blue
> And time is beginning to crawl
> I just might have to come see you
> Where teardrops fall

Although he'd already undergone at least three major turns in the road by the late Eighties, Dylan was well aware that he'd likely find himself back on the cross one day as a necessary step to some future turn further down the line.

If the 2006 song "Ain't Talkin'" (off *Modern Times*) is any indication, Dylan found himself between Gethsemane and Golgotha again as his body aged and he began shedding the suit of skin that would liberate his spirit from "this earthly domain of disappointment and pain," as he puts it in "When the Deal Goes Down," another song from *Modern Times*. In "Ain't Talkin'," the mystic garden evoked in the first and penultimate verses is the garden where Jesus' body was temporarily interred, in a grave donated by Joseph of Arimathea, who, incidentally, was one of several famous personages that Dylan told *Spin Magazine* in 1985 he'd most want to interview if he had a chance. The final two verses go:

As I walked out in the mystic garden
On a hot summer day, hot summer lawn
Excuse me, ma'am I beg your pardon
There's no one here, the gardener is gone

Ain't talkin', just walkin'
Up the road around the bend
Heart burnin', still yearnin'
In the last outback, at the world's end

Clinton Heylin points out the absent gardener is likely Jesus, and the woman (ma'am) a reference to Mary Magdalene, who the gospels describe (along with a small coterie of female disciples) looking for Jesus' body in the tomb the morning after his crucifixion. Here's how the story is told in Mark:

When they looked up, they saw that the stone, which was very large, had already been rolled back. As they entered the tomb, they saw a young man, dressed in a white robe, sitting on the right side; and they were alarmed; you are looking for Jesus of Nazareth, who was crucified. He has been raised; he is not here. (Mark 16:3–6)

Dylan's lyrics seem to approximate Mark insofar as the disciples react to the missing body through silence—"So they went out and fled from the tomb, for terror and amazement had seized them; and they said nothing to anyone, for they were afraid." The destiny of the poet/singer in this powerful and underrated song is to keep moving through an apocalyptic "outback," practicing—"a faith that's been long abandoned / Ain't no altars on this long and lonesome road." If redemption does exist in the lonesome toil of this world, it's more of a muted hope than a triumphant expectation.

Etiological Considerations

Across Chapters 2 and 3, I showed how Bob Dylan's more dramatic changes coincided with moments of developmental transition. Once again, these two rites of passage would have come as no surprise to either Victor Turner (1967) or Erik Erikson (1959), both of whom believed that change to identity was most likely during socially legitimized periods of transition from one psychosocial stage to another.

Unlike the aftermath of his motorcycle accident or his conversion to Christianity, the change explored in this chapter doesn't fit neatly into any classical theory of development. The theories of Piaget (1977), Freud (1905), Erikson (1959), and Kohlberg (1958) conceptualize human development as a sequential series of stages that progress from birth and through which individuals must successfully pass to achieve optimal psychosocial health. Script theorists like Rae Carlson (1981), on the other hand, make a convincing case for contextualist and/or dialectical perspectives that stress the role that environment and social relations play in the movement from one life period to another. If forceful enough, the activation of a nuclear script that had been previously activated during times of developmental transition could theoretically engender the onset of a new life stage, even in the absence of a socially recognized shift (e.g., the movement of childhood into adolescence).

The mid-Eighties for Dylan, once again, were a period of commercial flops, alcohol abuse, and personal angst. An episode of purposelessness prompted a familiar script of death and symbolic rebirth, just as it had before. According to the story he tells in *Chronicles*, his arm was dangerously mangled in a freak accident (a mortal threat of sorts), but he managed to regenerate (literally and figuratively) by tapping into the mysterious wisdom of the jazz/ blues greats Lonnie Johnson and Blind Gary Davis. The consequence of this reinvestment was tantamount to a conversion not unlike the one he experienced in 1978, minus any explicit mention of Jesus. However, the language Dylan used to explain this change was in many respects just as religious as the language he used after his Born Again experience. The old jazz singer is described as opening a window to his soul. "It was like parts of my psyche were being communicated to by angels," Dylan, again, writes. "There was a big fire in the fireplace and the wind was making it roar. The veil had lifted" (146). Such poetic imagery conveys an experience that many Christians call grace, in which a person is released from estrangement or suffering through a sudden and inexplicable sense of peace, purpose, and belongingness. The destiny script would retain Christian overtones of struggle and redemption ever after. It would also retain a new "scene of encounter," in which Dylan would find himself altered in significant ways after encountering a person or ghost with supernatural powers—whether it was Jesus himself in the Tucson hotel room, the old jazz singer in San Rafael, a memory of Lonnie Johnson, or the mysterious saxophonist in New Orleans whose face Dylan likens to a god's face. These are moments of Godly presence, or what theologians refer to as moments of "incarnation." In addition to connoting the union of

God and humankind in the person of Jesus, it can also refer more broadly to the dynamics of the holy on earth. Once again, I turn to T. S. Eliot's *Four Quartets* to express it poetically:

> These are only hints and guesses,
> Hints followed by guesses; and the rest
> Is prayer, observance, discipline, thought and action.
> The hint half guessed, the gift half understood, is Incarnation.
> Here the impossible union
> Of spheres of evidence is actual,
> Here the past and future
> Are conquered, and reconciled

Conclusion

A review of the destiny script over nearly twenty years of interviews and autobiographical writings reveals its enduring quality. According to Rae Carlson (1981), a case can be made for the magnification of a script when the following criteria are met: (1) evidence appears in more than one kind of data—for example, across interviews, memories, dreams, as well as in favorite songs, poems, novels, and in the biographies of other persons deemed interesting and/or significant by the subject; (2) there is the presence of analogs to the original scene (or scenes) across different developmental periods; (3) it contains combinations of various features of the original scene in the form of a shifting family of scenes; (4) it features the co-assembly of the original scene with later experiences that are both similar to and distinct from it; and (5) whereas scenes initially determine scripts, over time, the script determines the experience of scenes, shaping the experience of life according to its internal rules.

When used alone, script theory offers researchers a useful tool for understanding the structure, development, and dynamics of personality. But, of course, there is more to say about someone's personality than merely locating one of its many structures. What sociocultural forces, for example, influence the formation of a given script? And are these forces unique to the individual being studied or a defining experience of a specific group? And are they unique to a given historical period or present at the evolutionary level? An underexplored dimension of the research platform envisioned by Tomkins is the historico-cultural level of script analysis. Such analyses go beyond the descriptive by offerings cultural explanations. In Tomkins' own words:

Shall we, then, opt for a purely historical description of personality, or shall we cling to an a-historical account? I would suggest that the appropriate strategy is not an either-or, nor an indecisive eclecticism. The affect mechanism is innate and universal, but its structure lends itself to differential weighting of one affect over another, and of one locus of investment over another, and of one intensity over another. It is social, historically conditioned forces which play a decisive role in such options. Personality, therefore, is at once a partially closed and partially open system. Affect is to history as grammar is to semantics and pragmatics. It has as one consequence that the personality theorist must be as much at home with neurophysiology as with the study of comparative civilizations. (Tomkins, 1981, 452)

In the following chapter, I'll explore the "partially closed and partially open system" of Bob Dylan's personality by locating an especially salient scene from Dylan's youth growing up in Hibbing and exploring the historical forces that may have contributed to its deep and enduring internalization.

5 | WORLD GONE WRONG

I believe that ever since Adam and Eve got thrown out of the
garden, that the whole nature of the planet has been heading
in one direction—towards apocalypse.

—Bob Dylan, 1984

The origins of the threatening scene at the center of the
destiny script are both figuratively and literally "nuclear."
Dylan's birth on May 24, 1941, meant that his childhood,
adolescence, and adulthood coincided with the Cold War between the United States and the Soviet Union. For the first
time in history, humankind possessed the capacity to annihi-
late itself with its own technology. A *New York Times* editorial
published the day after Hiroshima referred to "an explosion in
men's minds as shattering as the obliteration of Hiroshima."
Based on his commentary over the years, the threat of nuclear
annihilation had significant and enduring effects. A few early
pages in *Chronicles* detail the pall of anxiety cast over his childhood. Dylan vividly recalls being trained as a grade-schooler,
at the age of ten, to take cover under his desk whenever the air
raid sirens sounded. In addition to being told that the Russians
could attack with nuclear bombs, the children of Hibbing were

informed that the enemy could parachute over the town at any moment.

> Living under a cloud of fear like this robs a child of his spirit. It's one thing to be afraid when someone's holding a shotgun on you, but it's another thing to be afraid of something that's just not quite real. There were a lot of folks around who took this threat seriously, though, and it rubbed off on you. It was easy to become a victim of their strange fantasy. . . . When the drill sirens went off, you had to lay under your desk facedown, not a muscle quivering and not make any noise. As if this could save you from the bombs dropping. The threat of annihilation was a scary thing. (Dylan, 2004, 29–30)

Dylan shares a similar memory in Martin Scorsese's *No Direction Home*: "Our reality was bleak to begin with," he states while reminiscing about his youth. "Our reality was fear. Any moment this black cloud would explode where everybody would be dead. They would show you at school how to dive for cover under your desk. We grew up with all of that so it created a sense of paranoia that was, I don't know, probably unforeseen."

This anxious memory is a salient one, and its reverberations can be felt through many of Dylan's self-reflections over the years. For example, he made a reference to the mass hysteria caused by "the bomb" in Nat Hentoff's 1964 *New Yorker* profile. And in a 2004 *Los Angeles Times* interview with Robert Hilburn, he brings up the bomb when asked to discuss the themes that moved him to write songs back when he was starting out. Explaining that the Korean War had just ended and that the Cold War was on the rise, Dylan evokes the image of a "cloud" to capture the zeitgeist of the times, which, much like the "cloud of fear" mentioned in the passage from *Chronicles* just quoted, evokes the familiar specter of a mushroom cloud. "That was a heavy cloud over everyone's head," Dylan tells Hilburn. "The communist thing was still big, and the civil rights movement was coming on. So there was lots to write about." He then elaborates on the anxiety created by the Cold War by sharing his memories of the Cuban missile crisis. "All I remember about the missile crisis is there were bulletins coming across on the radio, people listening in bars and cafes, and the scariest thing was that cities, like Houston and Atlanta, would have to be evacuated. That was pretty heavy."

The heaviness of Dylan's atomic fears was likely intensified by his knowledge of the Nazi Holocaust from his earliest years. As the descendent of eastern European Jewry, the reality of ethnic annihilation was something he was aware of. His mother's family ran a chain of movie theaters and witnessed horrifying newsreels that revealed mounds of dead bodies, emaciated living prisoners, and the various instruments of extermination. In addition to referencing the Holocaust in the 1962 satirical song "Talkin' John Birch Paranoid Blues" and mentioning it in *Chronicles*, it's present in one of his more rousing anti-war songs from 1963, "With God on Our Side." Debuted at the Town Hall in New York City on April 12, 1963, this lengthy anti-war jeremiad chronicles the murderous barbarisms of American domestic and foreign policy from the nineteenth century through a vision of World War III. The various wars and genocides included are unified by the fact that God was evoked in each case to justify the killing. The fifth verse goes:

> When the Second World War
> Came to an end
> We forgave the Germans
> And we were friends
> Though they murdered six million
> In the ovens they fried
> The Germans now too
> Have God on their side

Both sets of Dylan's grandparents had fled anti-Semitic hysteria in Eastern Europe several decades earlier. In his monumental study of Eastern European Jewish immigrants in America, Irving Howe (1976) documented a quiet but pervasive fear that was carried by many immigrant families that even in America anti-Semitism could become a genocidal problem. Dylan probably heard whispers of these fears from his extended family, a sizable portion of which lived in and around Duluth and Hibbing and whose stories of persecution and immigration undoubtedly influenced his emerging sense of uncertainty and danger.

Dylan's father, Abe (b. 1911), was the son of Jewish immigrants from Odessa who'd fled an anti-Semitic pogrom that left a thousand Jews murdered at the hands of fifty-thousand violent Czarists. Abe's father, Zigman, immigrated to America in 1907, traveling to the northern Minnesotan port town of Duluth. A bustling fishing port, Duluth had been a hub for what were once vast shipments of iron ore coming down from the mining towns of the Iron Range, which stretched to the northwest. Working as a street peddler, Zigman was able to save enough money to send for his Russian wife and three children. Three additional children, all boys, were born after the family was safely reunited in northern Minnesota.

Dylan's mother, Beatty (b. 1915), was the granddaughter of Ashkenazi Jews who'd fled Lithuania in 1905, the same year as the massacre in Odessa. The Stone/Edelstein family settled in and around Hibbing, running successful businesses (a string of movie theaters and a clothing store) that were utilized by the miners who made their livelihood in the giant strip-mine that the town was built around. Beatty's grandfather, "B. H." Edelstein, was devout orthodox Jew who lived to ninety-one, dying the very year his great-grandson moved to New York to pursue his musical dreams. Although Dylan's grandfathers died when he was fairly young, he knew his grandmothers well, especially his maternal grandmother who lived with him for a time growing up. In *Chronicles*, however, it's his paternal grandmother whom he describes in some detail. He writes of her as having only one leg and as having spent her working years as a seamstress. "She was a dark lady, smoked a pipe," remembers Dylan. "My grandmother's voice possessed a haunting accent—face always set in a half-despairing expression. Life for her hadn't been easy. She'd come to America from Odessa, a seaport town in southern Russia. It was a town not unlike Duluth, the same kind of temperament, climate and landscape and right on the edge of a big body of water" (Dylan, 2004, 93). In the same passage, he contradicts information on her death certificate stating Odessa as her birthplace by claiming she'd originally come from Turkey.

Whether or not this information is historically accurate (and it seems not to be), the story contributes to the "rootlessness" that underlies Dylan's shifting self-understandings. An echo of this can be found in his voiceover at the beginning *No Direction Home*: "I had ambitions to set out and find, like an Odyssey, going home somewhere, set out to find this home that I left a while back and couldn't remember exactly where it was, but I was on my way there, and encountering what I encountered on the way was how I envisioned it all. I didn't really have any ambition at all. . . . I was born very far from where I was supposed to be, so I'm on my way home."

His family's émigré past implanted a sense of spiritual homelessness that has stayed with him over the course of his life. As psychoanalytic theorist Julia Kristeva put it in her essay "Toccata and Fugue for a Foreigner" (1991): "The space of the foreigner is a moving train, a plane in flight, the very transition that precludes stopping . . . nothing binds them here. Always elsewhere, the foreigner belongs nowhere" (Kristeva, 1991, 8).

In the 1978 *Playboy* interview, Dylan explained his name change by appealing to the movements and migrations of his ancestors. "It's a common thing to change your name. Many people do it. People change their town, change their country. New appearances, new mannerisms. . . . But deep inside us we don't have a name. We have no name." When asked by Rosenbaum about his family name, Zimmerman, Dylan's response reflects sensitivity to the fact that the surname was itself only a few generations old: "My forebears were Russian. I don't know how they got a German name coming from Russia. Maybe they got their name coming off the boat or something. To make a big deal over somebody's name, you're liable to make a big deal about any little thing" (in Cott, 206).

The truth is that Dylan always felt ambivalent about Robert Allen Zimmerman, the name he'd been given at birth by Abe and Beatty. From his teenage years onward, he'd wear a whole laundry list of pseudonyms—including Elston Gunn, Alias, Jack Frost, Jack Fate, Elmer Johnson, Tedham Porterhouse, Robert Milkwood Thomas, Blind Boy Grunt, and Lucky and Boo Wilbury.

The fact that he changed his name and kept his Jewish identity secret during his early years in New York may suggest, among other motivations, the generational aftermath of cultural dislocation and the residual fear of anti-Semitism. In his masterful work, *The Bible in the Lyrics of Bob Dylan* (1985), the Dylan scholar and Biblical exegete Bert Cartwright also theorizes a relationship between Jewish identity and Dylan's personal theology of destruction and redemptive renewal:

> Yes, deep in his psyche remained the Jewish hope of history's fulfillment. First exploring the Bible's apocalyptic imagery from an artistic perspective of potent symbol, Dylan eventually adopted a quite literal understanding of the way God would get even with and, with his chosen few, prevail. Such an understanding of history wells up from the depths of a Jewish heritage that rehearsed each year within the family the liberating exodus of God's people from bondage. (Cartwright, 1985, 121–122)

Finally, it's important to note that Hibbing itself had an apocalyptic—or rather post-apocalyptic—quality to it environmentally. One of a cluster of mining towns that stretched to the northwest of Duluth, it had been stripped of its natural resources. In his colorfully impressionistic biography, *Who Is That Man?: In*

Search of the Real Bob Dylan (2012), David Dalton reflects upon the place where Robert Zimmerman grew up as follows: "Hibbing, Minnesota, is the site of the biggest man-made hole in the world, an existential allegory if ever there was one. Like a village in a fairy tale, Hibbing cannibalized itself in search of iron ore, undermining the town itself through relentless excavations. When the ore ran out in the '50s, so did the jobs, and the town underwent a depression from which it never entirely recovered" (Dalton, 2012, 8). The economic struggles of a town built around a mine robbed of its ore may have added fuel to the proverbial fire of Dylan's apocalyptic worldview. "What happens to a town after their livelihood is gone?" he asks rhetorically in *No Direction Home*. "It sort of blows away and is gone. That's the way it goes. Most of the land was either farmland or just completely scavenged by the mining companies."

Together, the threat of nuclear annihilation, family memories of anti-Semitism, the Holocaust, and the depleted ecology of the Iron Range instilled a persistent anxiety in the young Robert Zimmerman, filling his impressionable mind with images of extinction. He developed into a child who, according to his own reports, couldn't sit still for long, who was always chasing something that might lead him "into some more lit pace, some unknown land downriver." It was there that he hoped to find shelter from the storm.

The Apocalyptic, in Dylan's Words

To say that Bob Dylan has always been obsessed with death and disintegration (both personal and global) would be an understatement. Dylan's Minneapolis friend Gretel Hoffman claimed that one of Dylan's early original compositions was a pessimistic song about how he was nineteen and probably wasn't going to live to be twenty-one (Sounes, 2011, 61). The prospect of an early death seems to have rattled him continuously. In the nighttime airplane interview from Lincoln, Nebraska to Denver, Colorado with Robert Shelton in 1966, an exhausted twenty-five-year-old Dylan put it bluntly: "I have a death thing, I know. I have a suicidal thing, I know." Toward the end of the meandering interview, Dylan's frenzied thoughts enlarged death beyond the scope of his own mortality: "Hey, it's lonesome everyplace. The people that can't live with it, that can't accept it. . . . They are just going to blow up the world . . . and make things bad for everybody, only because they feel so out of place. . . . Everybody has that in common—they are all going to die."

Interpreters of Dylan's songs have long been aware of his fixation on the apocalypse—expressed in both geopolitical and then later in stark theological terms. Images of extinction populate early songs like "Let Me Die in My Footsteps," "Talkin' World War III Blues," and "A Hard Rain's a-Gonna Fall" and later songs like "Mississippi," the third track on the 2001 album *Love and Theft*. Originally intended for Dylan's 1963 album, *The Freewheelin' Bob Dylan*, "Let Me Die in My Footsteps" wasn't officially released until 1991. The song offers a nervously humorous response to the Cold War obsession with fallout shelters and air-raid drills. Dylan discussed its inspiration with *Playboy* in 1963, explaining that he'd witnessed the construction of a fallout shelter while "going through some town." As he watched, it struck him "sort of funny that they would concentrate so much on digging a hole underground when there were so many other things they should do in life. If nothing else, they could look at the sky, and walk around and live a little bit, instead of doing this immoral thing." In each refrain, the singer pleads to be left to die in his footsteps before he goes "down under the ground."

Ironic humor—a tried-and-true coping mechanism—is also present on the final track of the album, "Talkin' World War III Blues," which followed Woody Guthrie's talking blues form of reciting a rambling narrative over a simple and repetitive guitar line. The story begins with a trip to the psychiatrist's office to recount a convoluted dream about walking through a city amidst the rubble and ruin of a nuclear explosion. After asking for a stringbean at a fallout shelter and being turned away, Dylan calls out to a fellow survivor who runs off fearing that he is a communist. Lonely, he phones the woman who tells the time over the phone and is informed that when he hears the tone it will be three o'clock. The song concludes with the singer's psychiatrist interrupting his patient to inform him that he too has been plagued with a similar dream, the only difference being that it's him that's left alive in the dream and not his patient. The first three lines of the final verse encapsulate the fearfulness that simmers beneath the comedic surface of the song: "Well, now time passed and now it seems / Everybody's having them dreams / Everybody sees themselves walkin' around with no one else."

When it came time to mix and sequence *Freewheelin'* in the spring of 1963, "Talkin' World War III Blues" was dashed off impromptu on the final day of recording and "Let Me Die in My Footsteps" was replaced with the apocalyptic masterpiece "A Hard Rain's a-Gonna Fall," Dylan's best-known anthem of the Nuclear Age. In September 1962, the United States discovered Soviet missiles in striking distance of the mainland on the communist island of Cuba. President Kennedy announced publicly that he would take any and all necessary actions against the threat of Cuban aggression, which prompted Soviet leader Nikita Khrushchev to warn that an attack on Cuba would prompt a nuclear confrontation between the two superpowers. The Kennedy administration set up a naval blockade and warned the Soviets against the delivery of any offensive weapons to Cuba. Regardless, several Soviet ships supposedly attempted to run the blockade. As the standoff fomented into an international crisis, Dylan composed a harrowing song that conveyed his bleak vision of a post-apocalyptic world. The atomic rain that he imagined left trees dripping in blood, highways warped and twisted, oceans incapable of sustaining life, a woman engulfed in flames, and a baby encircled by wolves:

> Oh, what did you see, my blue-eyed son?
> Oh, what did you see, my darling young one?
> I saw a newborn baby with wild wolves all around it
> I saw a highway of diamonds with nobody on it
> I saw a black branch with blood that kept drippin'
> I saw a room full of men with their hammers a-bleedin'
> I saw a white ladder all covered with water
> I saw ten thousand talkers whose tongues were all broken
> I saw guns and sharp swords in the hands of young children
> And it's a hard, and it's a hard, it's a hard, it's a hard
> And it's a hard rain's a-gonna fall

Dylan would later explain that every line in the song was the first line of a song that he didn't think he'd have time to write.

Although he wrote and performed it three weeks prior to the blockade standoff, he informed Studs Terkel that it was written in direct response to the crisis. "It was during the Cuba trouble," said Dylan, "that blockade, I guess is the word. I was a little worried, maybe that's the word."

This worry was only amplified by the domestic and geopolitical violence that bloodied the decade following Dylan's arrival to New York in 1961. In *Chronicles*, he writes about hearing the news that France had exploded an atomic bomb in the Sahara Desert, how Ho Chi Minh had expelled the French from Vietnam, and how the Beat poet Gregory Corso's mushroom cloud-shaped poem "Bomb" captured the times more than Allen Ginsberg's "hydrogen jukebox" image from "Howl." In the final paragraph of the memoir, Dylan likens the national psyche of the time to the 1968 horror flick "Night of the Living Dead." He writes: "The road out would be treacherous, and I didn't know where it would lead but I followed it anyway. It was a strange world ahead that would unfold, a thunderhead of a world with jagged lighting edges" (Dylan, 2004, 293). As many who lived through these years will attest, the Kennedy assassination, the violent opposition to racial integration across many southern states, nuclear proliferation, and the escalation of the Vietnam War all emitted their share of thunder and lightning. Sensing that he was living during a seismic historical shift, Dylan describes some "research" he did in the New York Public Library after his arrival in New York, on America leading up to and through the Civil War, and he recalls thinking that his own historical moment resembled the country as it was a century earlier. "In some ways the Civil War would be a battle between two kinds of time," Dylan writes—adding that *his* time, although different in many ways, bore a resemblance to it in "some mysterious and traditional way. No just a little bit, but a lot" (Dylan, 2004, 86). He concludes this fascinating paragraph with a truncated iteration of the destiny script: "Back there, America was put on the cross, died and was resurrected. There was nothing synthetic about it. The godawful truth of that would be the all-consuming template behind everything that I would write" (Dylan, 2004, 86).[1]

A New World Is Coming

No psychological theorist has written on the violent excesses of the twentieth century more exhaustively than the psychiatrist and cofounder of psychohistory Robert J. Lifton. Over his long and distinguished academic career, Lifton has studied barbarism after barbarism—including medicalized killing during the Holocaust, the atomic bombings of Hiroshima and Nagasaki, Chinese thought reform, the Vietnam War, 9/11, and the U.S. War on Terror. In addition to exploring the impulses that drove the perpetrators of these atrocities, Lifton has written on the

1. Many commentators over the years have noticed this template in his songs. *Highway 61 Revisited*, for example, has been characterized by Davin Seay and Mary Neely, co-authors of a book tracing the gospel roots of rock music, as Dylan's exercise in "turning over rocks in the rubble at the end of time, prefiguring not just the demise of the sixties but some sort of ultimate extinguishment of hope, love, and body warmth" (Seay and Neely, 1986, 327–328)." Furthermore, an outstanding review of the apocalyptic dimensions of Dylan's catalogue can be found in chapter 4 of Michael J. Gilmore's excellent book *Tangled Up in the Bible: Bob Dylan & Scripture* (2004).

psychological consequences of mass violence in the lives of modern men and women.

In his 1979 book, *The Broken Connection*, Lifton theorized about how modern persons had become increasingly besieged by rootlessness and by images of extinction through mass media. The Holocaust, nuclear weapons, and the cultural displacements of an unprecedented number of immigrants, émigrés, and refugees had disrupted humankind's inner quest for continuous symbolic relationships to what had gone before and what would continue after our individual lives had run their course. This desire for death-transcending immortality, referred to by Lifton as *symbolic immortality*, was the psychological process through which the species dealt with the facticity of death. The process, however, had been disrupted by an accelerated pace of historical change and by the ever-present threat of future extinction. A foreboding feeling resulted, a threat to the vitality of the self or, in more extreme forms, from an anticipation of its disintegration.

Lifton (1979, 1993) has explained the rise of religious fundamentalism as a response, in part, to the fragmentation of our continuity with past and future. In other words, many modern persons have responded to the historical pressures of the twentieth and twenty-first centuries by gravitating to systems of belief (e.g., Millennial Christianity, Radical Islam, Hindu Nationalism, etc.) that offer identity coherence and the promise of eternal life beyond the finality of death. In the case of Christian fundamentalism, the notion of end times, as foretold in the Book of Revelation, is especially significant. In Lifton's words, "The promise of end time is the psychological fulcrum that holds together the fundamentalist self, and provides its controlling image. . . . In literalizing the Book of Revelation's account of the end of human history and Jesus' thousand-year reign on earth, the self also literalizes, and fixes in place, that version of immortality." Lifton explicitly connects Christian apocalyptic theology to Nuclear Age fear: "Subsuming nuclear-weapons-related imagery of extinction to the Book of Revelation provides the fundamentalist self with an important psychological means of coping with nuclear fear and futurelessness" (Lifton, 1993, 169–170).

Like many of his contemporaries whose lives during the Sixties and Seventies traveled the path of excess, Dylan's embrace of southern Californian Christianity at the Vineyard Fellowship makes sense. As Heylin and other biographers have pointed out, becoming Born Again at the moment that Dylan did was popular among musicians, especially for those struggling with drug and alcohol abuse, divorce, abandonment, hopelessness, and loss. Assistant Pastor Bill Dwyer, who baptized Dylan's girlfriend Mary Alice Artes and who taught a class that Dylan attended, characterized the appeal of the Vineyard message in an interview for Joel Gilbert's 2011 documentary, *Bob Dylan Revealed*: "There were a lot of people who were searching . . . a lot of baby boomers who had come through the '60s. They were not very happy with the way things went. The Vietnam War. Many of them were disillusioned. There was almost a sense of an apocalypse . . . that something was coming . . . that something needed to change. And so the message of Jesus, I think, really impacted people. It brought out this—*this* is what is missing in your life. And so we saw literally thousands of people decide to open their hearts to the Lord and invite him to take over their lives and lead them on."

For a period of time, Bob Dylan relished a rigid theological framework for understanding the sense of foreboding that had been with him for as long as he could remember. What's more, the Christian apocalyptic message had a silver lining: All those who believed by taking Christ into their hearts would be saved from ultimate destruction. In the words of Hal Lindsay, "As the battle of Armageddon reaches its awful climax and it appears that all life will be destroyed on earth—in this very moment Jesus Christ will return and save man from self-extinction" (Lindsay, 1970, 168). Given this life-restoring promise, it's no wonder that Dylan advertised *The Late Great Planet Earth* with the enthusiasm that he initially did, referencing it to friends and acquaintances excitedly, much as he would do a decade and a half later with Isaac Bashevis Singer's 1962 novel *The Slave*.

Dylan fervently believed the end was nigh and that the unfaithful and wicked would be judged. Belief in Jesus was the only path to salvation and that was that. Dylan's literalistic understanding of Christian eschatology was on full display during his first gospel tour. At one concert in the fall of '79, he openly witnessed to his audience:

You know we're living in the end times. . . . The scriptures say, "In the last days, perilous times shall be at hand. Men shall become lovers of their own selves. Blasphemous, heavy, and high-minded." . . . Take a look at the Middle East. We're heading for a war . . . I told you "The Times They Are a-Changin'" and they did. I said the answer was "Blowin' in the Wind" and it was. I'm telling you now Jesus is coming back, and He is! And there is no other way of salvation . . .

Jesus is coming back to set up His kingdom in Jerusalem for a thousand years.

When his audience expressed ambivalence or outright disdain, as they did on November 26, 1979, in Tempe, Arizona, Dylan patiently chided his hecklers with the paternalism of a pastor concerned over the spiritual welfare of his flock:

> What a rude bunch tonight, huh? You all know how to be real rude. You know about the spirit of the anti-Christ? Does anybody here know about that? Well, it's clear the anti-Christ is loose right now. . . . [T]here's many false deceivers running around these days. There's only one gospel. The Bible says anybody who preaches anything other than that one gospel, let him be accursed.

After having the lights turned up on the audience, he asked a pointedly eschatological question reminiscent of the Hebrew prophets: "How many people here are aware that we're living in the End of Times right now? How many people are aware of that?" The fact that the audience of rowdy college students continued to jeer him did little to diminish his fervor. Toward the end of the jeremiad just quoted from, Dylan shared the geopolitical evidence he'd read about in Lindsay's bestselling book:

> The real truth is that He's coming back already. And you just watch your newspapers. You're gonna see, maybe two years, maybe three years, five years from now, you just watch and see. Russia will come down and attack in the Middle East.

China's got an army of two hundred million people. They're gonna come down in the Middle East. There's gonna be a war called the Battle of Armageddon, which is like some war you never even dreamed about. And Christ will set up His kingdom. He will set up his kingdom and He'll rule it from Jerusalem. I know, as far out as that might seem, this is what the Bible says.

As the years and decades passed, Dylan continued to cite the Book of Revelation, even after disavowing ever being "born again," referring to the term as a media label. Although he distanced himself from the Vineyard Fellowship's brand of Christian spirituality by the early Eighties, his general fixation on end times remained a salient feature of his worldview.[2] All one really needs to do is listen to his music to catch this. The lyrics to "Jokerman," "When the Night Comes Falling from the Sky," "Things Have Changed," and "Mississippi" all reflect his belief that we're fast-approaching that "dreadful day." "Sky full of fire / pain pourin' down," Dylan croons over the rockabilly arrangement of "Mississippi," "Nothing you can sell me / I'll see you around."

It also occasionally came up as a topic during interviews. In 1984, for instance, he reported to Kurt Loder that he believed in the Book of Revelation and predicted the coming of a "new kingdom" in the ballpark of 200 years. "And the new

2. Lifton (1993) writes about how a commitment to fundamentalist precepts is often impermanent due to the inability to explain the perpetuation of pain, disarray, and death. Therefore, what begins as rigid ideological totalism often mellows over time into more malleable forms of spirituality.

kingdom that comes in, I mean, people can't even imagine what it's gonna be like." Later in the interview, Dylan became even more specific about where the battle of Armageddon was likely to take place: "The battle of Armageddon is specifically spelled out: where it will be fought, and if you wanna get technical, *when* it will be fought. And the battle of Armageddon definitely will be fought in the Middle East," he explained with certainty.

Thirteen years after the Loder interview, Dylan sat down with Jon Pareles to promote the 1997 Grammy-winning album *Time Out of Mind*. During the interview, Dylan described how he'd been captivated by an apocalyptic verse from the Bible during the period of time when he was writing and recording the album in Miami, Florida:

> A lot of the songs were written after the sun went down. And I like storms, I like staying up during a storm. I get very meditative sometimes, and this one phrase was going through my head: *"Work while the day lasts, because the night of death cometh when no man can work."* I don't recall where I heard it. I like preaching, I hear a lot of preaching, and I probably just heard it somewhere. Maybe it's in the Psalms, it beats me. But it wouldn't let me go. I was, like, what does this phrase mean? But it was at the forefront of my mind, for a long period of time, and I think a lot of that is instilled into this record. (Essential Interviews, 394)

Jesus says this in the Gospel of John (9:4): *"I must work the works of him who sent me while it is day; the night cometh, when no man can work."* Ironically, Dylan fell gravely ill shortly after the recording of the album due to a condition called pericarditis, an inflammation of the sac around the heart, which is a painful and potentially fatal if left untreated. Luckily, he was admitted to St. John's Hospital in Santa Monica and successfully treated. There's no doubt though that the sickness impelled him to work as tirelessly as he has through the intervening years. Like the Biblical prophets had, his never-ending tour crisscrossed the country and globe preaching the template of death and resurrection that underlay everything he would write.

Annihilation Anxiety

Lifton's understanding of modern *death anxiety* offers a helpful lens when understanding the unique characteristics of post-WWII consciousness. But what it doesn't account for are the different ways this anxiety can manifest psychologically. The psychoanalytic theorist Martin Hurvich, on the other hand, developed an analogous concept called *annihilation anxiety* and a theory that accounts for the diverse ways such affect can play out in different lives (Hurvich, 1989). Following Freud's thinking on anxiety, Hurvich investigated cases in which individuals develop an acute anticipation of danger and destruction related to memories of helplessness sustained during childhood. These early experiences dramatically increase future susceptibility to strong death anxiety that, unless properly managed, can threaten the cohesion of the self and the intactness of one's sense of identity.

What begins as overwhelming emotion in response to a real or imagined threat to biological survival expresses itself later in life as a wide range of recurrent fears: of being overwhelmed, devoured, of disintegrating at the levels of self or identity, of meaninglessness, mutilation, bodily injury, sickness, abandonment, and catastrophe. Both explicit threats (e.g., a physical accident) and implicit threats (e.g., the anticipation of danger, no matter how amorphous) can activate the anxiety. In this way, the experience can resemble a "flashback" in which overpowering and unprocessed emotions associated with an earlier trauma are relived. Like Tomkins's nuclear script, once amplified, the affect can be triggered by an array of stimuli—many of which might have an indirect structural relationship to the original event(s) associated with it. In the words of Hurvich and his colleague Norbert Freedman, "It [annihilation anxiety] may ebb and flow in intensity and undergo modification in form, signaling not only a process of change, but sometimes one of *transformation*" (Freedman and Hurvich, 2011, 89).

In Dylan's case, the terrifying experience of hearing the air-raid sirens as a ten-year-old and having to take cover under his desk left a lasting mark. The salience of this scene was amplified by its regularity and strengthened by his knowledge of the Holocaust and its genocidal implications for Jews. Images of Cold War-era extinction saturated the media, and Dylan was no doubt barraged by moribund bulletins he heard over the radio at night and by the scary anti-Soviet propaganda he witnessed on the newsreels shown before the Gregory Peck and James Dean movies he grew up watching in his uncle's chain of movie theaters. The threat of annihilation was such a scary and ubiquitous part of his generation's world that, for some, it crystalized into a cognitive/ affective schema that would be triggered during times of developmental transition, sickness, injury, and vulnerability.

Perhaps he relived the scary feelings associated with annihilation on the morning of Friday July 29, 1966, when he "crashed" his motorcycle outside of Woodstock—then again over a decade later in the painful wake of his divorce from Sara Lownds when, according to Howard Alk, death was in the air—and a further decade down the road after badly mangling his hand during the nadir of his career. Indeed, the "steady thrum of death" never seemed to be far away. And this "thrum" created a great sense of urgency in his life. In the face of an imminent death, it was essential to fulfill his purpose before it was too late. In 1965, he'd reflect upon his compulsion to write spontaneous Beat-style poetry by concluding that it was a fear of extinction that compelled him to do so: "I used to get scared that I wouldn't be around much longer, so I'd write my poems down on anything I could find—the backs of my albums, the back of Joan's [Baez] albums, anywhere I could find." The urgency behind this impulse also came up thirteen years later in the 1978 *Playboy* interview Dylan gave to promote *Renaldo and Clara*. He made clear that his need to perform was much more reflexive than conceptual: "...if you believe you have a purpose and a mission, and not much time to carry it out, you don't bother about those things." "Do you think you have a purpose and a mission?" asked Rosenbaum. "*Obviously*," Dylan responded.

This purpose and mission involved more than an irrepressible compulsion to compose and perform music. Its psychological underpinnings prompted an invention and reinvention of self as the

precarious circumstances of existence shifted. The most famous
of Dylan's incarnations, the mercurial poet-prophet of the 1960s,
was merely one iteration in what amounts to a long morphology.
Both on stage and off, Dylan has managed to bring together disparate and seemingly incompatible elements of identity and has
continually transformed these elements as if his life depended it—
which it did, and still does.

In his book, *The Protean Self: Human Resilience in an Age
of Fragmentation* (1993), Lifton postulated that the loss of historical continuity and fear of annihilation required people to
become increasingly protean. Named after the sea god Proteus,
who could take many different forms, the protean self was a re-
silient means of coping with the fragmentation of self and society in an age of uncertainty and violence. The proteanism of Bob
Dylan is linked to the ways he has engaged and subsumed musical and textual traditions into his sound *and* his sense of self.
In an article on Dylan's appropriations published in *Parnassus
Magazine*, Dylan scholar Mark Pollizzotti writes about how
reinvention is "the great natural resource of a nation that has
had to invent itself from whole cloth, and it is plentiful enough
to be used in myriad ways" (Pollizzotti, 2015, 18). Dylan, after
all, is not the first American character, historical or fictional,
to reinvent himself. Mark Twain's Huckleberry Finn, Herman
Melville's Confidence Man, F. Scott Fitzgerald's Jay Gatsby, not
to mention countless politicians and performers, invent and
reinvent themselves in various ways and with multiple motivations. Characters like Huck Finn (who Dylan immortalized in
the song "Huck's Tune") absorb a range of characters and re-
gional influences as they travel America in search of adventure

and for a deeper expression of self. It is also worth mentioning that Dylan's entire base of music, from Scottish ballads like "Tam Lin" and "Barbara Allen" to the Delta blues songs of Robert Johnson, is full of transmutations and metamorphoses. For example, lyrics from the sixteenth-century ballad "Tam Lin," which Clinton Heylin argues may have been a model for "Desolation Row," feature shape-changing everywhere:

> O, they will turn me in your arms to a newt or a snake
> But hold me tight and fear not, I am your baby's father
>
> And they will turn me in your arms into a lion bold
> But hold me tight and fear not and you will love your child
>
> And they will turn me in your arms into a naked knight
> But cloak me in your mantle and keep me out of sight

Having located annihilation anxiety as one motivation behind Dylan's changeability, the final chapter of this book will use some identity theory to postulate how Dylan's psyche drew upon the magical worlds of traditional American music to mold itself into a changing self-picture that has repeatedly enabled him—in his own words—"to crawl out from under the chaos and fly above it."

6 | THE AMERICAN PROTEUS

…on a whiskered lion's shape,
a serpent then; a leopard; a great boar;
then sousing water; then a tall green tree…

—Homer

As I mentioned in the introductory chapter, Dylan referred to himself as a "transfigured" person in the 2012 interview with Mikal Gilmore of *Rolling Stone*. Early in the conversation, he stands in response to a question about his public perception and grabs a nearby book that he supposes might be of interest to Gilmore. The book title is *Hell's Angel: The Life and Times of Sonny Barger and the Hells Angels Motorcycle Club*, by Sonny Barger. Dylan requests that Gilmore read the names of the coauthors: *Keith Zimmerman* and *Kent Zimmerman*—and then asks an esoteric question: "Do those names ring a bell? Do they look familiar? Do they? You wonder, 'What's that got to do with me?' But they do look familiar, don't they? And there's two of them there. Aren't there two? One's not enough? Right?" Sitting down and smiling, Dylan asks Gilmore to read a passage detailing a motorcycle accident in the Sixties that resulted in the death of someone also named Bobby Zimmerman.

"Yeah, poor Bobby," Dylan says afterward. "You know what this is called? It's called transfiguration. Have you ever heard of it?" Gilmore answers yes, and Dylan then refers to himself as someone who has been transfigured. "That's how I can still do what I do and write the songs I sing and just keep moving," he explains. "I couldn't go back and find Bobby in a million years," ostensibly referring to both the motorcyclist Bobby Zimmerman *and* to his former self. "Neither could you or anybody else on the face of the Earth. He's gone. If I could, I would go back. I'd like to go back. At this point in time, I would love to go back and find him, put out my hand. And tell him he's got a friend. But I can't. He's gone. He doesn't exist." After moving on to several other topics, Gilmore returns to transfiguration later in the interview. Pressed to explain what he means, Dylan answers analogically:

> And it makes perfect sense, because in the truth world, nothing does begin or end. You know, it's like things begin while something else is ending. There's never any sharp borderline or dividing line. We've talked about this. You know how we have dividing lines between countries. We have boundaries. Well, boundaries in the cosmological world don't really exist, any more than they do between night and day.

This view of selfhood is extraordinarily fluid. According to many leading personality theorists, our identities begin to crystalize through adolescence and early adulthood. And although shifting developmental demands and maturation will inspire and necessitate change at the levels of characteristic adaptations and narrative identity, we remain fairly stable across our life span at our dispositional cores, which many psychologists believe are the essence of personality. But transfigured individuals, at least according to Dylan, exist in a different category of space and time. "I'm not like too many others," Dylan says to Gilmore. "I'm only like another person who's been transfigured. How many people like that or like me do you know?"

The work of William James (1902) on conversion and the quantum change studies of William Miller and Janet C'deBaca (2001) suggest the possibility of a more radical depth of change experienced by a small but persistent number of people. A "quantum changer" may experience a sudden or gradual "vivid, surprising, benevolent, and enduring personal transformation" that influences a broad range of affective, cognitive, and behavioral dimensions. And there is even a subset of individuals who, like Dylan, undergo several significant changes over the course of life.

The goal of this book has not been to gauge the depth of Dylan's changes across the various levels of personality. Did Dylan change at the levels of dispositional traits and characteristic adaptations, or were his changes primarily on the narrative level? No one can answer that question—perhaps not even Dylan himself. We remain mysteries to ourselves, a reality present in the poignant lines from "Not Dark Yet"—

I was born here and I'll die here against my will
I know it looks like I'm moving, but I'm standing still
Every nerve in my body is so vacant and numb
I can't even remember what it was I came here to get away from . . .

My goal has been to search his self-descriptions for his sense of the roles these changes played in his development as an artist and person. Close reading of interviews and autobiographical writings reveals the presence of a redemptive script undergirding three of Dylan's major transformations: a change in the course of living that took place over the years that followed his mysterious motorcycle accident in 1966; his Born Again conversion experience in the final months of 1978; and his recommitment to writing and performing in 1987. The destiny script, as I choose to call it, consists of variations on a repetitive plotline:

> *I have lost my sense of identity and purpose—I feel anxious and vulnerable to death and destruction—I turn to the songs and artists of my youth for guidance—I feel a redeemed sense of self and purpose—I reflect upon the change and understand it as the process of developing into who I'm supposed to be.*

In the previous chapter, I concluded that these redemptive turns in the road were in part triggered by an overwhelming annihilation anxiety that intensified during periods of transition/angst. I traced this anxiety back to the nuclear air raid drills and Cold War paranoia of Dylan's youth in northern Minnesota. The redemptive mechanism of the script came in the form of a renewed sense of self and purpose that was consistently spawned by a religious relationship to the musical past. This relationship helped to assuage his deep-seated fear of disintegration by connecting him to a symbolic form of immortality through a range of new self-possibilities and their musical counterparts.

So far, my energy has been spent tracing the destiny script as it has morphed through time (Chapters 2–4) and theorizing about its historical origin (Chapter 5). But what sorts of psychological observations can be made about the new self-descriptions themselves? In other words, what can be said about the structure and content of the narrative self-descriptions that the destiny script helped to engender? Merely claiming that the musical past influenced Dylan's perennial redemptions isn't enough. Rather than speculate about the specific natures of the self-identities that followed his motorcycle accident in '66, Christian conversion in '78, and recommitment in '87, I will now offer a broad set of reflections on how the songs and artists from his time in front of the radio and record player as a child and teenager have factored into his transfigurations. These reflections reveal that the best place to look for Bob Dylan's identity is *in* his changes.

Narrative psychologists like Dan McAdams have long argued that people's identities are constructed through their narrative life stories. Narrative identity is the story a person attempts to keep going through the life span, an internalized and evolving narrative of self that weaves a reconstructed past and an imagined future into a relatively coherent whole. According to McAdams, the unique psychological fingerprints of people are present in the themes that dominate their life stories. McAdams has written in particular about how highly generative adults tend to narrate what he calls redemption sequences with frequency. Such sequences involve the movement in a scene from a negative situation emotionally to a positive result. They commonly involve "turning points" that use redemptive imagery to highlight transformative experiences. When I say Bob Dylan is best looked for in his changes, what I mean is that his redemptive turns in the road are the most salient and consistent theme in his life story. And so it follows that his self-proclaimed "constant state of becoming" is closer to his true identity than any of the individual personae he has assumed along the way.

"The Old Forms"

Dylan has said that he bases his melodies, which he characterizes as "very simple," on traditional songs. "My songs are based on old Protestant hymns or Carter Family songs or variations of the blues form," he explained to Robert Hilburn in 2004. "What happens is, I'll take a song I know and simply start playing it in my head. That's the way I meditate."

In a similar vein, the British classical composer and convert to Russian Orthodox Christianity, John Taverner, explained his relationship to traditional music in an interview. "It has taken me years to really understand what tradition is," Tavener is quoted as saying, "and to explain it to anyone else is difficult. People call it different things. In Islam, the Sufis call it 'the eye of the heart.' St. Augustine defined it as 'the intellective organ of the heart.' It's a different way of thinking about writing music. I used to fret over manuscripts and think, 'What am I going to do?' Now it's a question of going very quiet, emptying my mind of preconceived ideas and seeing what happens. It's not so much a question of finding my voice as finding *the* voice."

Compare this to the *New York Times* interview from 1997 quoted from in Chapters 1 and 2 in which Dylan discussed his relationship to the songs that inspired his youth:

> Those old songs are my lexicon and my prayer book. All my beliefs come out of those old songs, literally, anything from 'Let Me Rest on That Peaceful Mountain' to 'Keep on the Sunny Side.' You can find all my philosophy in those old songs. I believe in a God of time and space, but if people ask me about that, my impulse is to point them back toward those songs. I believe in Hank Williams singing 'I Saw the Light.' I've seen the light, too.

A similar sentiment is present throughout *Chronicles*. Folk songs like "Columbus Stockade," "Pastures of Plenty," and "If I Lose, Let Me Lose" were forms of life from which he derived palpable self-knowledge. He characterizes such songs as having offered him mental pictures worth more than anything he could possibly say. "Most of the other performers," he writes, "tried to put themselves across, rather than the song, but I didn't care about doing that. With me, it was about putting the song across" (Dylan, 2004, 18). This was because the songs were his grounding, his existential mooring, his method for crawling "out from under the chaos" and flying above it. On some very real level, the songs informed and shaped the person he was becoming. W. B. Yeats asks in the poem "Among School Children," "How can we know the dancer from the dance?" According to Sartre (1963), we can't. The significant projects of a person's life become a reflection and extension of that person, whether or not he or she recognizes him- or herself in the objectification.

It's historically significant that Dylan absorbed the musical past through the radio. This fact grants his many identities and musical masks a postmodern shape. In *The Protean Self* (1993), Lifton discusses the importance of mass media as a source for multiplicity. In addition to the anxiety-provoking way that radio broadcasts and television images saturated the post-World War II world with images of extinction, the mass media revolution also succeeded in expanding the self and stimulating people to think, feel, and act in a much more protean manner than was previously possible.[1] Although radio predated the level of media saturation that television created, the role it played in making other personalities, places, and times available to listeners shouldn't be underestimated.

The radio and phonograph have always held an oracular place within Dylan's worldview. The radio was where he went when he was in need of escape and comforting. Many of his childhood memories involve sitting or lying near the radio listening, allowing "the ghost of 'lectricity" (as he puts it in "Visions of Johanna") to entrance him. The rhythms of the music, the cadences of the lyrics, the themes evoked by the stories, and the colorful biographies of the singers coalesced within his consciousness, forming a mental universal of deeply internalized sounds, signifiers, and selves that Dylan would spend a life span channeling. Whether as refuge from the harsh winters of northern Minnesota, the terror

1. This notion has long been an interest of postmodern thinkers. According to the cultural anthropologist Richard Shweder (1991), many-sidedness and fragmentation are more useful ways of conceptualizing modern selfhood than the unified theories that have long dominated psychological theory.

of nuclear air raid drills, or the regimented expectations and work ethic of Abe, Dylan sought peace of mind from a wooden box with speakers and a dial. It was what he trusted and believed in most. "Back then when something was wrong the radio could lay hands on you and you'd be all right," Dylan, again, writes in *Chronicles*. Likewise, he told Sam Shepard in *A Short Life of Trouble* (1987) that he'd frequently fall asleep listening to the radio:

> I had lotsa dreams. Used to dream about things like Ava Gardner and Wild Bill Hickok. They were playin' cards, chasin' each other, and gettin' around. Sometimes I'd even be there in the dreams myself. Radio-station dreams. You know how, when you're a kid, you stay up late in bed, listening to the radio, and you sort of dream off the radio into sleep. That's how you used to fall asleep. That's when disc jockeys played whatever they felt like.

Robert Shelton also takes up the influence of the radio in *No Direction Home*. Similar to the preceding quotation, Dylan vividly described lying under his covers at night listening to stations out of Louisiana. The comforting role that the radio played is juxtaposed by Shelton to the increasing distance Dylan felt from his biological family:

> Bob took most of his journeys down the Mississippi late at night, when the air was cleaner. He often placed his radio under the covers to keep from waking anyone with sounds he caught from Shreveport or Little Rock. . . . In 1954, *McCall's Magazine* editorialized about togetherness, an idyllic portrait

of American family life updating *Saturday Evening Post* covers by Norman Rockwell, Andy Hardy films, *One Man's Family*. For Bob Dylan, who felt increasing separation from his family after he entered high school, togetherness was a midnight radio show from the South that said white and black music got along very well. (Shelton, 2010, 37–38)

Dylan scholars since Shelton haven't missed the radio as a source behind Dylan's identities and changes. In his book *Dylan Redeemed: From Highway 61 to Saved*, religion and philosophy professor Stephen Webb writes, "Dylan had just enough of one foot in the old world of acoustics to bring it into contact with the new world of amplification. Coming of age during this pivotal point in the history of sound, he learned how to channel voices from the past to disturb the deaf and wake the dead" (Webb, 2006, 102).

It was also from "the old world of acoustics" that he learned the secret alchemy of being "Bob Dylan." His immersion into this old world has always had a sacramental quality in the sense that it consistently guided him into an altered lived experience. Sacraments like baptism, communion, marriage, and holy orders, after all, usher the faithful into new and expanded realities that clarify and/or alter the nature and purpose of who they are.

During the final stages of writing this book, Dylan surprised his fans and followers, and the American entertainment industry as well, by showing up to accept an achievement award from the MusiCares organization, a charity that helps musicians in need. Early in his thirty-plus-minute speech, Dylan makes an intriguing reference. "I'm glad for my songs to be honored like this," he's quoted as saying. "But you know, they didn't get here by themselves.

It's been a long road and it's taken a lot of doing. These songs of mine, they're like mystery stories, the kind that Shakespeare saw when he was growing up. I think you could trace what I do back that far. They were on the fringes then, and I think they're on the fringes now. And they sound like they've been on the hard ground."

The reference to "mystery stories," or *mystery plays* to be exact, is an intriguing one. And given Dylan's considerable erudition, it's likely that he meant something by it. Mystery plays were a popular form of medieval drama that reenacted scenes from the Bible in cycles that coincided with liturgical feasts and holy days. In addition to offering an illiterate population direct knowledge of Biblical stories, they were also sacramental in character. In an age when sacraments were generally kept at some distance from the laity, the audience at a mystery play might experience full, conscious participation in the Biblical events as they were performed. Just as the Catholic doctrine of transubstantiation requires a parishioner to receive the bread and wine ("the accidents") as the actual body and blood of Christ, the spectator of a mystery play wouldn't merely watch the actors (comprised of specific guilds acting out specific scenes) playing the roles of Adam and Eve, or Pontius Pilate and Jesus, but might feel intimately involved in the reality of the stories and personages depicted.

"The Old Forms" as Symbols of the Self

The self, according to Lifton (1993), is defined by its capacity for symbolization. Everything we encounter through the life span is absorbed and reconstituted by the mind into a shifting network of cognitions, narratives, affective impulses, and behaviors. Although there are genetic and dispositional perimeters within which people function, who we are is at least partially determined by how our psyches consciously and unconsciously process the relationships we forge, the texts we read, the things we experience, the places we go, and—for people like Dylan—the things we hear. This manner of conceptualizing the self involves a fluid give and take between the internal (psychic) and the external (environmental) worlds and rejects older, deterministic theories of identity that stress inner stability across time.

Along these lines, Dylan explained to Sam Shepard that when he was young he'd frequently dream about music. "I mean, sometimes I'd hear a guy sing a tune and I'd imagine the guy himself. What's the guy himself like? Like Hank Williams or Buddy Holly or John Lee Hooker. You'd hear a line like *black snake moan* or *Mississippi Flood*—you could see yourself waist-high in muddy water." Lifton argues that visions like these, if potent enough, can get projected into functional symbols of *who* one is. A feeling of personal destiny, from this perspective, might involve the process of externalizing an internalized vision of the self—or as Dylan himself put it—"a feeling you have that you know something about yourself that nobody else does. The picture you have in your mind of what you're about *will* come true."

The evolving self-picture that Dylan has had in his mind of what he's about is indebted to no one source, but to a rich amalgamation of singers and their musical worlds. In the 1978 interview with *Playboy*'s Ron Rosenbaum, Dylan opened up when asked about the music he was listening to in his private life. He answered—"the same old black-and-blue blues. Tommy McClennan, Lightnin' Hopkins, the Carter Family, the early Carlyles. I listen to Big Maceo, Robert Johnson. Once in a while, I listen to Woody Guthrie again. Among the more recent people, Fred McDowell, Gary Stewart. I like Memphis Minnie a whole lot. Blind Willie McTell. I like bluegrass music. . . ."

In the same interview, he references visions he had as a child growing up in Hibbing. "I had some amazing projections when I was a kid, but not since then. And those visions have been strong enough to keep me going through today." *What were those visions like*, asks Rosenbaum? "They were a feeling of wonder," he responds. "I projected myself toward what I might personally, humanly do in terms of creating any kinds of reality." He then goes on to explain that Hibbing's brutally long winters played a significant role inducing "amazing hallucinogenic experiences," some of which involved redemptive imaginings that he was somebody else—or at least destined to become someone other than the eldest son of Abe and Beatty Zimmerman.

The annihilation anxiety that gnawed away at his spirit hastened the creation of a series of projected subselves who were impervious to death and stagnation. Each of these subselves was created from one or more influences, and each resonated for a time within the authentic key signature of who he believed he was.

The Imago

As a young man, Dylan repeatedly expressed fascination with Arthur Rimbaud's saying, "Je est un auture," translated "I *am* another." In addition to the tropes of mistaken and/or lost identity that pepper his songs (e.g., "Ballad of a Thin Man" or "Queen Jane

Approximately"), the theme of being one thing and then becoming something else is present in compositions like "Desolation Row" with its cosmology of transmutations, "Isis" off the 1976 album *Desire*, or the deeply affecting "Every Grain of Sand," originally released as the closing song on the gospel-influenced *Shot of Love* from 1981. In the deeply affecting penultimate verse, Dylan sings of redemption after a period of pain, struggle, and alienation:

> I have gone from rags to riches in the sorrow of the night
> In the violence of a summer's dream, in the chill of a wintry light
> In the bitter dance of loneliness fading into space
> In the broken mirror of innocence on each forgotten face

Given the morphologies of selves inside Dylan's songs and life, another possible way of conceptualizing his experience of self is through the concept of *imagoes*. An imago is a psychological metaphor for an internalized subself—based on a specific person, especially a parent, mentor, or hero figure—that becomes an idealized projection of one's identity. Identity typically encompasses many of these recurring characters, each with its own unique set of attributes. Dylan's changeability and numerous alter egos—Blind Boy Grunt, Jack Fate, and countless others—signal that the concept of imagoes offers a valuable tool for mapping out the topsy-turvy nature of his many projected self-possibilities. Recall that Dylan informed Shepard that when listening to the radio in Hibbing he'd imagine the singer as faceless. "I'd fill in the face," he purportedly said. And in one of his many interviews with Robert Shelton, he explicitly connected his musical influences to the changes that had marked his life:

> It was just like an adolescent, you know. When you need somebody to latch onto, you find somebody to latch onto. I did it with so many people, that's why I went through so many changes. I wrote a lot of stuff like Hank Williams, but I never grasped why his songs were so catchy or so classic. As for Presley, I don't know anybody my age that did not sing like him, at one time or another. Or Buddy Holly. (Dylan in Shelton, 2010, 38)

There are a number of striking illustrations of how deeply Dylan's heroes and their musical worlds have influenced him at times over his career. Three of many examples are Woody Guthrie (1912–67), Blind Willie McTell (1898–1959), and Buddy Holly (1936–59)—encompassing, respectively, Dylan's investment in the folk/ballad, Delta blues, and early rock-n-roll musical canons. The self-identities he fashioned in response to their examples weren't mere reflections, but self-projections guided largely by the ways that their songs and personal stories made him feel about who he was and what he was meant to do in the world.

The Woody Guthrie Imago

Born in Okemah, Oklahoma, in 1912, Woodrow Wilson Guthrie displayed an early aptitude for music and learned to play guitar and sing. Growing up in Oklahoma and Texas, he became one of thousands of itinerant laborers, referred to as "Okies," who traveled west to California in search of opportunity during the Dust Bowl era. This experience inspired a lifelong interest in the welfare of working people and an abiding love for the natural world. A "rambler and gambler," Guthrie enjoyed drinking, chasing women, and stood for no systematic political worldview other than freedom and equality for all: black and white, rich and poor, young and old. After stints playing music on the radio in California and Washington State, he moved east to New York City to join his friend Pete Seeger as a core member of the Almanac Singers—and then spent the years of World War II travelling the country with Lead Belly, Sonny Terry, and Cisco Houston before joining the Merchant Marines for a short stint at sea.

In addition to his unique style of playing and singing, Guthrie's wanderlust, scrappy working-class persona, and social consciousness were an inspiration to the younger more politically active singer-songwriters associated with the folk revival of the late Fifties and early Sixties. His recordings, radio broadcasts, and live performances also popularized earlier traditions like the Anglo-Irish ballad of Appalachia and the blues of the Mississippi delta. About Guthrie's legacy, Alan Lomax once wrote: "he inherited the folk tradition of the last American frontier (western Oklahoma) and during his incessant wandering across the US he has recomposed this tradition into contemporary folk ballads about the lives of the American working class. . . . No modern American poet or folk singer has made a more significant contribution to our culture."

Guthrie's musical style and personal example galvanized a nineteen-year-old Bob Dylan. Introduced to Guthrie's more popular songs at some point before 1960, Dylan's interest quickly blossomed into an outright obsession. But it was the experience of reading a Minneapolis friend's 1949 first-edition paperback copy of Guthrie's *Bound for Glory* that led to the birth of a new persona. Dylan's first major "transfiguration" was taking place. In fact, the personal changes that he underwent in some ways resembled the quantum changes he would experience in 1966, 1978, and 1987. His Minnesotan girlfriend of the time, Bonnie Beecher, who, incidentally, was the inspiration behind his song "Girl from the North Country," is quoted by Clinton Heylin on the topic of her boyfriend's rather abrupt change after spending the summer of 1960 in and around Denver, Colorado: "He came back [to Minneapolis] talking with a real thick Oklahoma accent and wearing a cowboy hat and boots. He was into Woody Guthrie in a big, big way. . . . At the time it seemed ludicrous and pretentious and foolish, but now I see it as allowing a greater Bob Dylan to come out" (Heylin, 2003, 47). Other friends commented on how his formerly melodious singing voice morphed into a twang and nasal version of Woody's voice and how he began playing a harmonica mounted on a metal neck brace as well. There were even occasions when a stoned or drunk Bob demanded that friends refer to him as Woody. This obsession with a guru-like figure impelled him to leave Minneapolis to find his diminished hero in Morristown, New Jersey, a relatively easy bus ride from the New York City Port Authority Bus Terminal.[2]

2. While in New York, Dylan kept up his Woody shtick. In her 2008 memoir of Greenwich Village, Dylan's great love of his early New York years, Suze Rotolo, describes how his fashion sensibilities, personal mannerism, and musical repertoire all attempted to channel his hero. "Much time was spent in front of the mirror trying on one wrinkled article of clothing after another, until it all came together to look as if Bob had just gotten up and thrown something on," Rotolo remembers. "Image meant everything" (Rotolo, 2008, 9).

In *Chronicles*, Dylan reminisces about the hold that Guthrie's music and persona had on him during his final months in Minneapolis. He describes listening at an acquaintance's home to a set of double-sided 78 records of Guthrie performing solo and feeling literally stunned by the intensity of the melodies and the poetry of Guthrie's lyrics. The songs were beyond categorization and conveyed "the infinite sweep of humanity." The language he uses to characterize the effect that the music had on him exceeds mere appreciation:

> That day I listened all afternoon to Guthrie as if in a trance and I felt like I had discovered some essence of self-command, that I was in the internal pocket of the system feeling more like myself than ever before. A voice in my head said, "So this is the game." I could sing all these songs, every single one of them and they were all that I wanted to sing. It was like I had been in the dark and someone had turned on the main switch of a lightning conductor" (Dylan, 2004, 244–245).

In particular, Dylan was captivated by the self-presentation that Guthrie offered across the loosely autobiographical pages of *Bound for Glory*, which he read "like a hurricane." He was mesmerized by Guthrie's rambling ways. "Woody's songs were having that big an effect on me," Dylan writes, "an influence on every move I made, what I ate and how I dressed, who I wanted to know, who I didn't" (Dylan, 2004, 247). He even felt that Guthrie and he were related: "Even from a distance and having never seen the man, I could perceive his face with a clearness. He looks not unlike my father in my father's early days." A Freudian, of course, would likely perceive such a statement as reflective of a search for a father figure to model himself after, especially considering the strained relationship that Dylan had with Abe. Regardless of the underlying motivation, Guthrie's music and persona granted Dylan a sense of identity that quickly superseded his identity as Robert Zimmerman. "The folk and blues tunes had already given me my proper concept of culture, and now with Guthrie's songs my heart and mind had been sent into another cosmological place of that culture entirely" (Dylan, 2004, 248), Dylan writes. It was *in* this other "cosmological place" that he felt more like himself than ever before. But the Woody persona was only temporary, an important signpost on a journey to an even deeper expression of self.

The Blind Willie McTell Imago

Bob Dylan began growing out of his "Woody" phase shortly after meeting his legend at Greystone Park Psychiatric Hospital. Gradually, a persona more indebted to early rock-n-roll and to the Mississippi delta began coming into focus. His appreciation for the blues and its bluesmen is well documented.[3] One of his earliest blues heroes was Lead Belly, whom he discovered shortly before leaving for college. Black musicians were also given occasional airplay, in addition to being available to an extent on vinyl recordings from the so-called "race record" era. Dylan recalls staying up to

3. Being a Jew whose extended family had known ethnic persecution and anti-Semitism, he had always felt a spiritual kinship to African American culture. Many of his musical heroes were black, as have been many of the women he has dated over the decades.

two or three in the morning listening to Muddy Waters, John Lee Hooker, Jimmy Reed, and Howlin' Wolf. As he has explained on multiple occasions, there was something about the sound of the songs that called him in. "It was the sound that got to me. It wasn't who it was. It was the sound of it. I began listening to the radio. I began getting bored being there [Hibbing]."

Similar to the Guthrie persona in *Bound for Glory*, many of the black musicians who Dylan was listening to and dreaming about were itinerant workers and performers who traveled from place to place playing for audiences at saloons, hotels, medicine shows, religious camp meetings, county fairs, on early race records, and then later on hotel room recordings for eager ethnomusicologists such as Harry Smith and Alan Lomax. Dylan felt a strong, nearly ancestral calling to their painful struggles and expressive triumphs. The cultural traditions of African Americans were and are the most influential and consistent sources behind Dylan's musical creations, in addition to having informed many aspects of his life off the stage. In the words of Dylan scholar David Yaffe, "Dylan's racial crossover (referring to *Another Side of Bob Dylan*, recorded in 1964) was not only musical and political but, at various times in his life, religious and sexual" (Yaffe, 2011, 70).

He was performing blues as part of his repertoire by 1960. By June 1961, he'd become proficient enough on blues harmonica playing to be hired as a one-time session player for a Harry Belafonte's recording of "Midnight Special." And the original title for his second album, *The Freewheelin' Bob Dylan* (1963), was *Bob Dylan's Blues*. And it's also telling that the title of his masterpiece, *Highway 61 Revisited* (1965), pays homage to a frequently recorded blues number called "Highway 61." Whether it's his apocryphal story of learning the blues from Black Mance Lipscomb during an imaginary stint in Texas, or being taught an esoteric style of guitar playing by Lonnie Johnson, or his decision to name his 2001 album *Love and Theft* after Eric Lott's 1993 academic study of black-face minstrelsy, the blues are everywhere one cares to look in Dylan's life.

In *Dylan in America* (2010), Princeton University historian Sean Wilentz explores the influence of one particular blues legend, Blind Willie McTell. Immortalized on a deeply affecting outtake from *Infidels* (1983) appropriately titled "Blind Willie McTell" (a song that many Dylan writers have ranked as his finest composition of the Eighties), McTell's sound and story were deeply inspirational. Unlike performers like Lead Belly, McTell was absent from the *Anthology of American Folk Music* and so it's likely that, as a young man, Dylan only heard dribs and drabs of McTell's recorded work. Although a few LPs and biographical sketches (e.g., a 1977 interview published by McTell's widow Kate McTell in the British magazine *Blues Unlimited*) were available during the Sixties and Seventies, the full extent of his recorded work wasn't loosed into the world until 1983, the same year that Dylan recorded his moving tribute.

The similarities between the two men are striking, to say the least. McTell, for instance, also spun fantastical tales about his early years growing up in Statesboro, Georgia. Born blind and named William Samuel McTier, he exhibited early musical talent and attended the Georgia Academy for the Blind in Macon, where he honed his skills as an outstanding guitarist, singer, and composer. A few years after leaving the Academy, he moved to the metropolis of Atlanta and changed his name from McTier to McTell.[4]

Over a period of twenty years, McTell made a name for himself around Georgia, playing regular gigs at several spots and attracting a local following at each. McTell couldn't sit still for long and informed his wife Kate that he was "born to ramble," and he proved it by playing all manner of venue in all manner of place, tirelessly driven to develop his craft on the road and make as much money as possible doing so. Hardly wedded exclusively to the blues, McTell also played an array of styles including spirituals and Tin Pan Alley hits, in addition to hillbilly standards that he picked up from other bluesmen working the various southern entertainment circuits. McTell, like Dylan, became a deeply religious man with a formidable knowledge of scripture, which he committed to memory through his knowledge of braille, but he was also no stranger to booze and prostitutes. And he was meticulous in his appearance, wearing a fashionable suit, tie, and billed cap in addition to keeping a well-groomed mustache not unlike the one Dylan began wearing sometime around the release of *Love and Theft* in 2001. Wilentz concludes the final chapter of his book with a brief reflection on these similarities:

> Dylan also in some ways spiritually resembled Blind Willie McTell, travelling endlessly, performing endlessly, sharp to the wiles of the world, taking things from everywhere but fixing them up his own way, composing new songs and

4. The change may have sounded more suitable for a professional guitarist and singer.

performing old ones that were sometimes sacred and some-times secular, but neither black nor white, up nor down—and that had reference to everybody. (Wilentz, 2010, 335)

The Buddy Holly Imago

Before Dylan had heard of Lead Belly, white musicians like Elvis Presley and Bill Haley were on the airwaves popularizing black rhythm-and-blues hits like Ivory Joe Hunter's "Shake, Rattle and Roll." The electric rock musicians of Dylan's early to mid-teenage years were both Black and White. Bill Haley, Elvis, Buddy Holly, Bobby Vee, Little Richard, Chuck Berry, Jimmy Reed, B. B. King, and others inspired a young Bobby Zimmerman to form his own rock-n-roll groups that played at high school talent shows, dances, and occasionally at local legion halls: the Shadow Blasters, the Golden Chords, and the Satin Tones.[5]

A young Bobby Zimmerman had been fortunate enough to see Buddy Holly's penultimate performance in late January with Link Wray at the Duluth Armory before the airplane crash on a snowy night in early February of 1959 that killed him, Richie Valens, P. J. Richardson (the Big Bopper), and the man who piloted the small chartered plane. The highlight of the concert for Dylan was when Buddy Holly looked straight into his eyes. It would happen again, a quantum leap between two people, a potent theme of Dylan's life—his first personal encounter with Woody Guthrie in 1961

---

5. The fact of these early experiences playing in electric rock ensembles falsifies the popular perception that Dylan "went electric" at the 1965 Newport Folk Festival.

at Greystone Park Psychiatric Hospital in New Jersey . . . or his guitar lesson with Lonnie Johnson in New York City . . . or his personal encounter with Jesus in Tucson, Arizona . . . or the jazz singer who helped revive his lagging spirits during rehearsals with The Grateful Dead in San Rafael . . . or his mysterious late-night glimpse of the saxophonist during the *Oh Mercy* sessions who reminded him of Reverend Gary Davis. The comments Dylan made in 1993 on the influence of the fathers of the Delta blues seem just as applicable to the encounters just cited. "Those vibes will carry into you forever, really, so it's like those people, they're still here to me. They're not ghosts of the past or anything. They're continually there."

The electrifying moment he experienced as Buddy Holly stared at him would loom large ever after. He kept talking about it off and on through much of his life, even recounting the memory in 1997 during a short acceptance speech he gave after winning a Grammy for the critically acclaimed *Time Out of Mind*:

> I just want to say, one time when I was about sixteen or seventeen years old, I went to see Buddy Holly play at the Duluth National Guard Armory . . . I was three feet away from him . . . and he looked at me. And I just have some sort of feeling that he was—I don't know how or why—but I know he was with us all the time we were making this record.

During the recording of *Time Out of Mind* in Miami, Dylan met with reminders of Buddy Holly nearly continually. He explained to the magazine *Guitar World* in 1999 that the sounds of rock-n-roll records from the Fifties had inspired the sound and attitude of the album:

> Those records were made a long time ago, and you know, truthfully, records that were made in that day and age all were good. They all had some magic to them because the technology didn't go beyond what the artist was doing. It was a lot easier to get excellence back in those days on a record than it is now. . . . The high priority is technology now. It's not the artist or the art. It's the technology that is coming through. That's what makes *Time Out of Mind* . . . it doesn't take itself seriously, but then again, the sound is very significant to that record.

And the ghost of Buddy Holly was at the center of it all, like Jesus had been around the time Dylan was finishing his world tour in '78, and like the bards and balladeers of the Scottish and Appalachian hills had been during his recovery from the motor-cycle accident in '66. Here's how he explained Holly's ubiquitous presence in an interview:

> While we were recording, every place I turned there was Buddy Holly. You know what I mean? It was one of those things. Every place you turned. You walked down a hallway and you heard Buddy Holly records like "That'll Be the Day." Then you'd get in the car to go over to the studio and "Rave On" would be playing. Then you'd walk into this studio and someone's playing a cassette of "It's So Easy." And this would happen day after day after day. Phrases of Buddy Holly songs

would just come out of nowhere. It was spooky. But after we recorded and left, you know, it stayed in our minds. Well, Buddy Holly's spirit must have been someplace, hastening this record in a kind of way.

Thoughts of Holly were only a half step from thoughts of mortality. The young pop star's death in February 1959 shook Dylan in a similar way that Elvis' death would eighteen years later. "I was burned with death all around me," Dylan said in 1965 of his years in Hibbing following Holly's tragic death. An associative connection between Holly and mortality seems even more probable given the meanings behind a Biblical verse (cited in Chapter 5) that also influenced the recording of *Time Out of Mind*. "I get very meditative sometimes," Dylan, again, told Jon Pareles shortly after the album's release, "and this one phrase was going through my head: *'Work while the day lasts, because the night of death cometh when no man can work.'* I don't recall where I heard it. I like preaching, I hear a lot of preaching, and I probably just heard it somewhere. Maybe it's in the Psalms, it beats me. But it wouldn't let me go. I was, like, what does this phrase mean? But it was at the forefront of my mind, for a long period of time, and I think a lot of that is instilled into this record." Perhaps Dylan imagined himself as an aging Buddy Holly, as an incarnation of Holly who'd narrowly escaped death so that he could carry out the work he'd been put on earth to do before the night of death.

According to many of the critics who reviewed the album, mortality—whether Holly's, Dylan's own, or everybody's—saturated the compositions. It suggested the reality of an aging man (Dylan, by the way, was closing in on sixty)—driven by desire, anguish, longing, and a raging mind—walking miles and miles of dusky terrain, haunted by the ghosts of his past and reminders of death, perhaps nowhere more evident than in "Not Dark Yet." "I've still got the scars that the sun didn't heal," Dylan sings, referring perhaps to the sun literally, or else the hurting parts that even Jesus couldn't redeem. "There's not even room enough to be anywhere," he continues, "It's not dark yet, but it's getting there."

These poignant lyrics turned out to be prophetic. Shortly after recording *Time Out of Mind*, Dylan began experiencing chest pain that became increasingly worse. At the behest of his daughter, he checked himself into a Santa Monica hospital for a cardiac evaluation. As it turns out, he had developed a potentially fatal case of histoplasmosis. Consequently, his upcoming tour was cancelled, and he lived for a time with excruciating pain and labored breathing. "It was something called histoplasmosis that came from just accidentally inhaling a bunch of stuff that was out on one of the rivers by where I live (referring to his farmhouse in Minnesota)," Dylan told *Guitar World*. "Maybe one month, or two or three days out of the year, the banks around the river get all mucky, and then wind blows a bunch of the swirling mess in the air. I happened to inhale a bunch of that. That's what made me sick. It went into my heart area, but it wasn't anything really attacking my heart." As ever, "the steady thrust of death" was looking over its shoulder at him. And what was his therapy? What else but getting back on tour with his band as soon as he found the physical strength.

According to his biographers, the health scare impelled him to lose some excess weight by watching his diet, quitting smoking, and exercising more so that he could continue to live out his end of the bargain he mentioned to Ed Bradley. The recording of *Time Out of Mind*, after all, had felt like another new beginning. When asked by *Guitar World* whether the album would've been "a good final chapter" had his medical condition resulted in death, Dylan demurred. "No, I don't think so. I think we were just starting with getting my identifiable sound onto the disc . . . I didn't feel like it was an ending to anything. I thought it was more the beginning."

A Protean Self and Its Stories

In *The Protean Self* (1993), Robert Lifton argues that modern people have coped with the breakup of tradition and the hovering threat of extinction by becoming more "protean."[6] He contends that since the mid-twentieth century, psychological health has hinged on personal malleability and the capacity for transformation. Lifton points to a literary source, Joyce's *Ulysses*, in his attempt to define proteanism. "The process is laid bare in James Joyce's rendition of Ulysses, surely the greatest protean literary journey of the twentieth century. Joyce's 'Proteus' episode . . . portrays 'a world dominated by metamorphoses which continually produce new centers of meaning'" (Lifton, 1993, 50). Although impermanent, these centers are capable of generating a sense of personal cohesion and continuity with the past and future. The protean self moves through the lifecycle linking "identity elements" and "subselves," creating and

6. Proteus was the Greek sea god of many forms who appears at a key moment in Homer's *Odyssey*.

recreating a pattern that engenders a unique experience of purpose, fate, and historical trajectory. Early in the book, Lifton summarizes the defining features of the phenomenon:

> Central to its function is a capacity for bringing together disparate and seemingly incompatible elements of identity and involvement in what I call "odd combinations," and for continuous transformation of these elements. At the same time, the protean self must cope with, and sometimes even cultivate, feelings of fatherlessness and homelessness, associated with shifts in authority and mentorship. One may take on the psychology of a survivor and undergo symbolic forms of death and rebirth that contribute further to shapeshifting. At the same time, one always seeks a degree of form, grounding, and cohesion. (Lifton, 1993, 5)

This summary encapsulates the very aspects of Bob Dylan's personality that this book has tried to make sense of. In addition to the symbolic forms of death and rebirth examined in Chapters 2, 3, and 4, Dylan has a long history of "odd combinations," whether his musical incarnations—his marriage of folk music and electric rock into the hybrid genre of folk-rock, or his identity as a modern American minstrel on later albums like *Love and Theft* (2001) on which he seamlessly combines folk influences with rockabilly, in addition to sweet, old-time radio melodies from the 1930s and 1940s—or the bevy of "odd combinations" that permeate his life. A self-proclaimed adherer to "Biblical values," his rampant womanizing, self-absorption, and issues with substance abuse indicate a more antinomian way of being. Or consider his syncretistic infusion of Judaism and Christianity. His claim that there was no substantive division between who he was as a Jew and who he became as a Christian makes sense when considered through the lens of Lifton's theory.

Furthermore, Dylan has always combined (and recombined) his imagoes into an evolving milieu of identities. The personae and songs channeled from the Invisible Republic have collided, gathered, and dispersed in a shifting constellation of internalized self-conceptions. Saying where one ends and another begins isn't possible because they are enmeshed. Like the spectral figure that T. S. Eliot encounters on the burning streets of London in "Little Gidding," Dylan's imagoes are *compound* ghosts. In his *Rolling Thunder Logbook*, Sam Shepard puts it like this—"Dylan has invented himself. He's made himself up from scratch. That is, from the things he had around him and inside him. Dylan is an invention of this own mind. The point isn't to figure him out but to take him in. He's not the first one to have invented himself, but he's the first one to have invented Dylan."

As for themes of fatherlessness and homelessness, Dylan's "never ending tour," chronic restlessness, and lifelong search for creative mentors make him a protean wanderer of the first order, a true wayfaring stranger. Little Richard, Hank Williams, Buddy Holly, Woody Guthrie, Charley Patton, Muddy Waters, the Reverend Gary Davis, Dock Boggs, and Dave Van Ronk among others were influential mentors from whom he learned and absorbed songs, styles, values, and personal mannerisms. But he never stayed put for long before moving on, although always taking what he desired and making it his own. For this reason, many of his living mentors (Ramblin' Jack Elliott and Dave Van

Ronk come to mind) felt ripped off and discarded once they ceased to be of interest or use.[7]

The fragmented personal stories that Dylan has shared on the topic of these transfigurations contain two primary narratives that are reconciled through the destiny script. According to the identity theorist Gary Gregg (2007), people typically move between a repertoire of distinct and at times contradictory self-narratives, or "discourses," about who they are and what it means for them to be in the world. Within Dylan's life story, one narrative laments a world gone terribly wrong. Haunted by displacement, deceit, danger, isolation, and death, the self wanders lost and threatened. The second narrative involves a story of redemptive self-discovery inspired by "the old forms" and the mythopoeic universe of love, divinity, transformation, and resilience that these "forms" engender.

Using the conceptual language of Gregg (2007), the second self-representation is an alternative identity-defining discourse that symbolically recalibrates the core-level tension of annihilation anxiety into the redeemed identity of a singer-songwriter driven by the drums of destiny to reinvent himself through song. Gregg would likely interpret the nuclear script explored in this book as a repetitious movement back and forth between two contrary self-representations managed by the integrating plotline of a redemption story. The two tropes at the center of this story are transfiguration and destiny—*changing as a means of becoming who one was*

7. Dylan's dismissive behavior toward others—whether enemies, friends, or former lovers—comes up frequently in biographies. He can be gregarious and generous, but a good deal of the time he has been brusque, cold, and downright cruel to people.

meant to be. Consequently, differentiating Dylan's identities misses the fact that, early in his life, he adopted an ever-changing identity of "constant creation" that has remained relatively stable over time.[8]

The phenomenon of proteanism is nothing new. Greek myths, Buddhist parables and sutras, the Ramayana, Scottish ballads, shamanism, and the lives of everyday people are full of transmutations of every kind. Notwithstanding possible genetic, dispositional, and sociopolitical constraints that may limit transformation, the human species is highly adaptable and capable of significant flux throughout the life span. A life like the one lived by Bob Dylan suggests that, for some, there may be a greater deal of fluidity and multiplicity across time than for others. The interesting psychological task is to determine the historical forces and psychodynamic structures behind the inclination for change. All at once, Dylan was someone, no one, and virtually everyone. In other words, Dylan was change.

Conclusion

What this book has demonstrated is the extent to which Atomic Age anxiety, along with the technology of the radio, impelled a pattern of self-reinvention and generativity in the life of a hugely influential artist. These claims are modest contributions when it comes to the unfinalizable work of understanding *who* someone is and *why*. In her 1967 essay called "Dylan," the writer and journalist

8. There is little doubt that his immense wealth and celebrity have given him the agency, space, and means to change as frequently and as profoundly as he has. The socioeconomics behind proteanism cannot be denied.

Nora Ephron summed up Dylan's personality as follows: "Friends describe [him] as shy and defensive, hyped up, careless of his health, a bit scared by fame, unmaterialistic but shrewd about money, a professional absorbed in his craft." To this thumbnail sketch we might add a deep-seated fear of death and a pattern of moving from chaos to redemption and back again. Perhaps "the rest is silence," as Hamlet famously says to Horatio in Act V of *Hamlet*.

Kinney's *The Dylanologists* (2014) explores the psychology that leads individuals to write books about Dylan's personal life, to follow him out on tour year after year, or to haunt the places he has been, desperate to feel the same contagion that inspired such masterpieces as "Visions of Johanna" or "Simple Twist of Fate." In this way, Dylan's celebrity more closely resembles the life of a living Hindu saint than a rock star. Kinney implies that the obsession might very well be specific to a generation of baby boomers who needed Dylan to be much more than the song-and-dance man that he once half-seriously described himself as. Dylan has always resented the constant and invasive attempts to discover the meaning of his life. As he put it, again, in 2001: "These so-called connoisseurs of Bob Dylan music, I don't feel they know a thing, or have any inkling of who I am and what I'm about. I know they think they do, and yet it's ludicrous, it's humorous, and sad." Maybe the more compelling, not to mention respectful, story behind who Bob Dylan is allows us to explore what his works and days teach us about having lived in the ragged edge of history that produced him. Such a story, needless to say, will take time to tell. But that's okay, because his songs will keep people interested long after the man born Robert Allen Zimmerman returns to the obscurity from which he came.

NOTES ON SOURCES

A choice was made not to congest the text with citations or an excessive number of footnotes. Across the pages that follow, I want to provide some information on *some* of the source materials for each chapter.

There were several books, mainly biographies, that were relied on to reconstruct Dylan's life. For each chapter, I refer to these sources (listed below) through the use of the author's initials (CH for Clinton Heylin, and so on). For Dylan's interviews, I drew from an array of source materials. My main sources were Jonathan Cott, ed., *Bob Dylan: The Essential Interviews* (2006), and James Ellison, ed., *Younger than that Now: The Collected Interviews with Bob Dylan* (2004), and *Rolling Stone's* Special Collectors Edition *Bob Dylan: 40 Years of Rolling Stone Interviews* (2013). These sources will be indicated with Bob Dylan's initials followed by the initials of the editors (BD in JC for Bob Dylan in Jonathan Cott, and so on). A significant amount of documentary evidence was taken from Bob Dylan's volume of memoirs, *Chronicles: Volume One* (2004), which will be hereafter denoted by Bob Dylan's initials alone (BD). Michael Gray, ed., *The Bob Dylan Encyclopedia* (2008), was a staple for the purposes of cross-referencing and filling out biographical details. For other essential references, I provide bibliographic information in the chapter-by-chapter breakdown that follows this list.

BD: Bob Dylan, *Chronicles: Volume One* (New York: Simon & Schuster, 2004)

CH: Clinton Heylin, *Bob Dylan: Behind the Shades Revisited* (New York: HarperCollins, 2003)

DD: David Dalton, *Who Is that Man?* (New York: Hyperion, 2012)

DME: Daniel Mark Epstein, *The Ballad of Bob Dylan: A Portrait* (New York: Harper Perennial, 2012)

HS: Howard Sounes, *Down the Highway: The Life of Bob Dylan* (New York: Grove Press, 2011)

JC: Jonathan Cott, ed., *Bob Dylan: The Essential Interviews* (New York: Wenner Books, 2006)

JE: James Ellison, ed., *Younger than that Now: The Collected Interviews with Bob Dylan* (New York: Thunder's Mouth Press, 2004)

MG: Michael Gray, ed., *The Bob Dylan Encyclopedia* (New York: Continuum, 2008)

RS: Robert Shelton, *No Direction Home: The Life and Music of Bob Dylan* (New York: Backbeat Books, 2010)

PROLOGUE: A CASE FOR THIS PSYCHOBIOGRAPHY

I am greatly indebted to the work of William Todd Schultz, ed., *Handbook of Psychobiography* (New York: Oxford University Press, 2015), especially the chapter "Introducing Psychobiography" (pp. 3–18). I also drew from William Todd Schultz, "Introduction: A Short Psychobiography Primer" in *Tiny Terror: Why Truman Capote (Almost) Wrote Answered Prayers* (New York: Oxford University Press, 2011).

Gordon Allport, *Letters from Jenny* (New York: Harcourt, 1965), provided a useful template for accessing a life through a nonlinear and episodic form of autobiographical documentation.

Conceptually, I also relied heavily on Jean-Paul Sartre, *The Search for Method* (New York: Vintage Books, 1968), as well as David Kinney, *The Dylanologists: Adventures in the Land of Bob* (New York: Simon & Schuster, 2014).

Freud's correspondence to Jung on the topic of using psychoanalysis to analyze art in *The Freud/Jung Letters* (New York: Princeton University Press, 1994) was helpful in my decision to focus on Dylan's narrative self-descriptions as opposed to focusing on his lyrics. Facing a Pandora's box of meanings, motives, and origins, any "psychological" interpretation of the lyrics may have led to interpretive reductionism, which I wanted to avoid. Similarly, Freud advises Jung against psychological reductionism when analyzing creative writings.

CHAPTER I: MASKED AND ANONYMOUS

The epigraph to this chapter is from Ali Shariati's book on Hajj.

My choice to focus on Dylan's personal and artistic morphology was largely a response to *No Direction Home*, directed by Martin Scorsese (Paramount Home Video, 2005, DVD, 208 min.). In one of the interviews, Dylan explains that, as an artist, he can't ever feel as if he's "arrived somewhere" and that he has to "be constantly in a state of becoming." Also influential was the movie *I'm Not There*, directed by Todd Haynes; screenplay by Todd Haynes and Oren Moverman (two-disc collector's edition, Weinstein Company, 2007, DVD, 135 min.).

Erik Erikson believed that it wasn't unusual for creative people to reexamine and renegotiate their identities more often and intensely than other people. In his influential work, *Identity: Youth and Crisis* (1968), Erikson examined the relationship between identity and creativity in brief analyses of George Bernard Shaw and William James. His psychosocial theory of identity development across the lifespan argued for change in accordance with biological maturation and shifting social roles. *Idenity and the Life Cycle* (1959) argues for eight stages of development from infancy through old age.

Although many creative people experience significant personal and artistic changes, Dylan considers himself unique in terms of the fundamental nature of his major changes. He refers to himself as a "transfigured" person in a 2012 interview with *Rolling Stone*'s Mikal Gilmore (*RS 1166*, September 27, 2012). In the same interview, Dylan also connects his experience as a "transfigured" person to a feeling of personal destiny.

Mainstream academic personality psychology tends to doubt fundamental adult change across the life span due to the predominance of genetic and trait epistemologies in contemporary personality theories.

In his foundational work, *The Principles of Psychology* (New York: Henry Holt and Company, 1890), William James suggested that personality was "set in plaster" by early adulthood.

Personality psychologists Dan McAdams and Jennifer Pals have drawn on extensive empirical research to contend that individuals remain relatively constant at the level of dispositional traits but malleable at other levels. In their 2006 article, "A New Big Five: Fundamental Principles for an Integrative Science of Personality" (*American Psychologist*, *61*, pp. 204–217), they conceptualize personality as five interrelated levels—an individual's unique variation on the evolutionary design for human nature expressed as a pattern of dispositional traits, characteristic adaptations, and self-defining narratives situated in specific sociocultural contexts. According to the authors' vast survey of research, characteristic adaptions and life narratives are the most probable levels to show change over time.

I contrast McAdams and Pals's conception of personality with the phenomenological work of William James, *The Varieties of Religious Experience* (London: Longmans, Green & Co., 1902). James explored two types of religious conversion: a willful or *volitional type* and a more sudden and affective type called the *type by self-surrender*. According to his estimates, both could lead to life-altering shifts in the "habitual center" of "personal energy."

James's work on conversion phenomena is bolstered by William R. Miller and Janet C'deBaca, *Quantum change: When Epiphanies and Sudden Insights Transform Ordinary Lives* (New York: Guilford Press, 2001).

My knowledge of the research behind adult personality change was greatly enhanced by a collection of essays published by the American Psychological Association (APA) in 1997: Todd F. Heatherton and Joel L. Weinberger, *Can Personality Change?* (New York: APA Press, 1997). I cite many of its studies and theories in the present book.

My reference to self-defining memories draws from Pavel Baglov and Jefferson Singer's 2004 article, "Four dimensions of self-defining memories (specificity, meaning, content, and affect) and their relationships to self-restraint, distress, and repressive defensiveness" (*Journal of Personality*, *72* (3), 481–511).

- The subsection of Chapter 1 called "The Bob Dylan Legend" drew from timelines and significant life events generally agreed upon by BD, BD in JC, DME, MG, CH, RS, and HS. Of particular help were the collected essays of the American musicologist Greil Marcus published in *Bob Dylan by Greil Marcus: 1968–2010* (New York: Public Affairs Press, 2010).
- The allegations of plagiarism that have trailed Dylan since his 2001 album *Love and Theft* are chronicled by HS, pp. 440–452.
- An outstanding overview of the conceptual foundations of phenomenological psychology, and specifically interpretive phenomenological analysis (IPA), can be found in Larkin, M., Watts, S., and Clifton, E. (2006), "Giving Voice and Making Sense in Interpretative Phenomenological Analysis," *Qualitative Research in Psychology*, *3*(2), 102–120.
- The conceptual language I employ when writing about my practice of examining a life from a double perspective of faith and suspicion is taken from Ruthellen Josselson's 2004 article, "The hermeneutics of faith and the hermeneutics of suspicion." *Narrative Inquiry*, *14*(1), 2004, 1–28.
- My use of Silvan Tomkins's script theory throughout the book draws heavily from E. Virginia Demos (ed.), *Exploring Affect: The Selected Writings of Silvan S. Tomkins* (New York: Cambridge University Press, 1995), pp. 295–388. I also draw upon Dan McAdams's use of script theory in his book *The Redemptive Self: Stories Americans Live By* (New York: Oxford University Press, 2013).
- My understanding of script theory was aided by Tim Kasser's psychobiography on John Lennon. *Lucy in the Mind of Lennon* (New York: Oxford University Press, 2013).
- The double hermeneutics of Paul Ricoeur (regressive vs. progressive) was developed in his groundbreaking monograph *Freud and Philosophy: An Essay on Interpretation* (New Haven: Yale University Press, 1970).
- Freud's 1910 monograph on Leonard da Vinci, *Leonardo da Vinci and a Memory of His Childhood*, is considered the first psychobiography dedicated to the life of an artist.

CHAPTER 2: THE MOTORCYCLE CRACK UP

The epigraph to this chapter is from Saul Bellow's 1964 novel *Herzog*.

Biographical overviews of the events leading up to Bob Dylan's supposed motorcycle accident (July 1966) can be found in DD, pp. 161–181; CH, pp. 166–280; and HS, pp. 189–221.

The interviews examined in the subsection titled "The Script" can be found in BD in JC, pp. 139–160, 347–365; and *RS 1166*, September 27, 2012.

Many of the interview excerpts and biographical details distributed through the subsection titled "The Progressive Project" were taken from Greil Marcus, *The Old Weird America: The World of Bob Dylan's Basement Tapes* (New York: Picador, 1997). Critical appraisals of Dylan's creative work in the years immediately following the accident can be found in DD, pp. 183–237; CH, pp. 281–338; and HS, pp. 222–256. Also extremely informative was Mikal Gilmore's 2013 article "Dylan's Missing Years" in *Rolling Stone* (RS 1191, September 12, 2013).

To explore the developmental dynamics behind this change I drew upon the anthropological work of Victor Turner, "Betwixt and Between: The Liminal Period in Rites de Passage," in *Symposium on New Approaches to the Study of Religion: Proceedings of the 1964 Annual Spring Meeting of the American Ethnological Society*, edited by J. Helm (Seattle: American Ethnological Society), pp. 4–20.

My thoughts on the psychology of addiction were informed by XXX Jefferson Singer's book *Messege in a Bottle: Stories of Men and Addiction* (XXX: Free Press, 1997)

Erik Erikson's *Identity and the Life Cycle* (1959) informed my thinking on Dylan's identity struggles after his "accident."

CHAPTER 3: SAVED

Biographical overviews of the events leading up to Bob Dylan's Jesus experience in 1978 can be found in DD, pp. 279–310; CH, pp. 450–490; and HS, pp. 307–397. In particular, Paul Williams, *What Happened?* (San Francisco: Entwhistle Books, 1980), provided me with an array of psychological insights. Williams follow-up essays "One Year Later" and "Bob

Dylan and Death" published in Paul Williams, *Bob Dylan: Watching the River Flow* (New York: Omnibus Press, 1996), pp. 134–151, 158–161, were also illuminating.

As in Chapter 1, my use Silvan Tomkins's script theory draws from E. Virginia Demos (ed.), *Exploring Affect: The Selected Writings of Silvan S. Tomkins* (New York: Cambridge University Press, 1995), pp. 295–388.

The interviews examined in the subsection titled "The Script" can be found in BD in JC, pp. 271–308; in addition to Scott T. Marshall, *Restless Pilgrim: The Spiritual Journey of Bob Dylan* (New York: Relevant Media Group, 2002), pp. 21–60.

Many of the interview excerpts and biographical details distributed through the subsection titled "The Progressive Project" were taken from Michael J. Gilmour, *The Gospel According to Bob Dylan* (Louisville: Westminster John Knox Press, 2011), pp. 67–112. Critical appraisals of Dylan's creative work in the years immediately following the accident can be found in DD, pp. 289–323; CH, pp. 490–526; and HS, pp. 352–390.

Reference is also made to Hal Lindsey's bestselling *The Late Great Planet Earth* (Grand Rapids: Zonderban, 1970) due to its influence on Dylan.

My framing of Dylan's Jesus experience and the changes it engendered in his life, nattative, and music was greatly aided by the work of Peter G. Stromberg, Language and Self-Transformation: a study of the Christian Conversion Narrative (New York: Cambridge University Press, 1993), and also Lewis R. Rambo, *Understanding Religion Conversion* (New Haven: Yale University Press, 1993).

In the subsection entitled etiological considerations, a reference is made to Ruthellen Josselson's book *Revising Herself: The Story of Women's Identity From College to Midlife* (New York: Oxford University Press, 1996). I drew from Josselson's thinking on the correlation between divorce and identity change.

CHAPTER 4: THE RECOMMITMENT

The epigraph to this chapter is from Abraham Maslow's 1954 work *Motivation and Personality*.

Biographical overviews of the events leading up to Bob Dylan's recommitment experience in 1987 can be found in BD, pp. 145–151; CH, pp. 527–609; and HS, pp. 368–384.

The interviews and autobiographical writings examined in the subsection titled "The Script" can be found in BD, pp. 151–221; and RS882, November 22, 2001.

Critical appraisals of Dylan's creative work in the years immediately following the accident can be found in BD, pp. 151–221; CH, pp. 610–706; and HS, pp. 398–476. I also learned a good deal from David Yaffe, *Bob Dylan: Like a Complete Unknown* (New Haven: Yale University Press, 2011).

My thoughts on transfiguration were informed by Bishop Kallistos Ware's classic *The Orthodox Way* (Crestwood, New York: St Vladimir's Seminary Press, 1979).

My encapsulation of Tomkins's Script Theory at the end of the chapter was guided by an outstanding summary of Tomkins's theories published by Rae Carlson (1981), "Studies in Script Theory: I. Adult Analogues of a Childhood Nuclear Scene," *Journal of Personality and Social Psychology*, *40*(3), 501–510.

CHAPTER 5: WORLD GONE WRONG

The opening of this chapter draws heavily upon BD, pp. 25–35; the opening minutes of *No Direction Home* (2006); and BD in JC, pp. 13–28.

A brief history of Dylan's parents and both sets of grandparents can be found in BD in JC, pp. 199–236; RS, pp. 26–52; and HS, pp. 19–21. Dylan also elaborates (and partly fictionalizes) his family's fragmented history in *Chronicles: Volume One*, pp. 230–246.

I am indebted to the work of Bert Cartwright, *The Bible in the Lyrics of Bob Dylan* (Lancashire: Wanted Man, 1985) for the connection I make between Dylan's apocalyptic worldview and Jewish eschatology.

To learn more about the Eastern European Jewish immigrant experience, I drew upon Irving Howe's landmark book *World of Our Fathers: the journey of the east European to Amerian and the life they found and made* (New York: Hartcourt Brace, 1976).

A reference is made to Julia Kristeva's *Strangers to Ourselves* (New York: Columbia University Press, 1991).

A colorful description of the Hibbing of Dylan's youth is offered by DD, pp. 7–12. The chapter, "World Gone Wrong: Bob Dylan's Apocalyptic Vision" in Michael J. Gilmore, *Tangled Up in the Bible: Bob Dylan & Scripture* (London: Continuum, 2004) examined the depth and frequency of apocalyptic imagery in Dylan's lyrics, which helped to fortify my focus on eschatology.

In apocalyptic imagery in Highway 61 Revisited was explored by Davin Seay and Mary Neely in their book *Stairway to Heaven: The Spiritual Roots of Rock 'N' Roll* (New York: Ballantine Books, 1986).

My indebtedness to the lifework of Robert J. Lifton is significant. His two long theoretical works, *The Broken Connection: On Death and the Continuity of Life* (New York: Simon & Schuster, 1979), and *The Protean Self: Human Resilience in an Age of Fragmentation* (Chicago: University of Chicago Books, 1993), are at the forefront of my analyses.

On the suggestion of one of my blind reviewers during the proposal stage of this project, I developed my thinking about nuclear-related death threat by engaging with the "annihilation anxiety" theories of the psychoanalytic theorist Martin Hurvich (1989), Traumatic moment, basic dangers and annihilation anxiety, *Psychoanalytic Psychology*, 6(3), 309–323.

To better understand the concept of annihilation anxiety I consulted: Freedman, Norbert., Marvin Hurvich, Rhonda Ward, Jesse D. Geller, and Joan Hoffenberg. *Another Kind of Evidence: Studies On Internalization, Annihilation Anxiety, and Progressive Symbolization in the Psychoanalytic Process* (London: Karnac, 2011).

Mark Pollizzotti's 2015 *Parnassus* essay "Love and Theft: Dylan's appropriations" helped me clarify my thinking on Dylan's appropriations.

CHAPTER 6: THE AMERICAN PROTEUS

This chapter begins with an extended meditation on the 2012 interview with *Rolling Stone*'s Mikal Gilmore (*RS 1166*, September 27, 2012).

In particular, three Bob Dylan interviews (from 1991, 1997, and 2004) informed my development of the subsection titled "The Old Forms." See BD in JC, pp. 367–390, 391–396, and 429–438. The material on Bob Dylan and the radio in RS, p. 37, helped me hypothesize the role that the radio played in Dylan's emerging sense of self-identity.

A reference is made to Jean-Paul Satre's book *Search for a Method* (New York: Alfred A. Knopf, 1968).

My thinking on the influence of the radio on Bob Dylan's identity was aided by Richard Shweder's *Thinking Through Culture: Expeditions in Cultural Psychology* (Cambridge, Massachusetts: Harvard University Press, 1991).

I quoted Dylan's reflection on the radio during his youth in Hibbing from Sam Shepard's one act play *Short Life of Trouble*, published in Esquire Magazine (1987). Stephen Webb's book *Dylan Redeemed: From Highway 61 to Saved* (London, Bloomsbury Publishing, 2006).

My understanding of Imagoes was fortified by Jefferson Singer (2013, August), Living in the amber cloud: A life story analysis of a heroin addict, *Qualitative Psychology*, *1*(S), 33–48.

I drew upon CH, pp. 47–56, 59–72 for information regarding Woody Guthrie and Bob Dylan's youthful obsession with the older folk hero. I also drew upon Suze Rotolo's memoir *A Freewheelin' Time: A Memoir of Greenwich Village in the Sixties* (New York: Broadway Books, 2008).

My understanding of Blind Willie McTell was fortified by Sean Wilentz, *Bob Dylan in America* (New York: Doubleday, 2010), pp. 172–206.

Dylan's relationship to the life and work of Buddy Holly is well encapsulated by DME, pp. 56–57, 179, 294, and 333.

The identity theory of Gary Gregg that I introduced at the end of the chapter can be found in Gary S. Gregg, *Culture and Identity in a Muslim Society* (New York: Oxford University Press, 2007), pp. 14–56.

INDEX